Christ Died at Notting Hill

THE WAY OF THE CROSS TODAY

The Bible Reading Fellowship

BRF encourages regular, informed Bible-reading as a means of renewal in the churches.

BRF issues various series of regular Bible readings with explanatory notes.

BRF publishes introductory booklets on Bible-reading, group study guides, training aids, audio-visual material, etc.

Write or call now for full list of publications and services.

The Bible Reading Fellowship

St Michael's House
2 Elizabeth Street
London SW1W 9RQ
Tel: 01-730 9181

PO Box M
Winter Park
Florida 32790
USA

All Saints Church
1 Bonney Street
Ainslie   ACT 2602
Australia

MICHAEL HOLLINGS

Christ Died
at Notting Hill

THE WAY OF THE CROSS TODAY

the bible reading fellowship

The Bible Reading Fellowship
St Michael's House
2 Elizabeth Street
London SW1W 9RQ

First published 1985

The scripture quotations are from:
The Revised Standard Version © 1952, 1957 and 1971 by Division of Christian Education of
the National Council of the Churches of Christ in the United States of America

British Library CIP data

Hollings, Michael
    Christ died at Notting Hill : the Way of
    the Cross today.
    1. Lent—Prayer-books and devotions
    I. Title
    242'.2   BV85
    ISBN 0–900164–65–4

Printed by Bocardo & Church Army Press Ltd., Cowley, Oxford, England

CONTENTS

PREFACE

Whenever I put words together on paper, I become indebted to a number of people who rally round to tidy up my spelling and grammar, to type my illegible handwriting accurately and clearly, and to untangle some of my less than literary constructions.

First and foremost, Sister Joseph Camac brings her eighty-year-old mind and eye to bear with far greater clarity than I do mine at twenty years younger. She is tireless, painstaking, but most importantly of all she is both kind and patient. Joan Cooley has carefully checked and re-typed the manuscript, making necessary and pertinent suggestions on the way. I am in debt to them both.

Secondly, I would like to thank the Bible Reading Fellowship and particularly Raymond Hammer for prodding me into undertaking the meditations. This has helped me to meditate a little more and to put down thoughts which otherwise simply buzz round my head.

Finally and with enduring gratitude for peace, space and an atmosphere of prayer, I thank Etta Gullick, in whose home on the Isle of Man much of the work was done.

Michael Hollings

St Mary of the Angels,
Moorhouse Road, London W2
St James, the Apostle, 1984

Scripture quotations are, for the most part, from the Revised Standard Version. Psalm references include the liturgical number in square brackets; the verse numbering follows that in the Bible.

FOREWORDS

True companions make all the difference to a journey. They draw our attention to landmarks we otherwise might pass by; they show us the way, encourage us, criticize our false starts, make demands on us, entertain us and offer us the friendship that carries weary legs that little bit further.

Our first companion in the way of the Cross is the Lord Jesus himself, who shows us the way to the Father. He has already taken this pilgrimage, conquered death and come to the 'glory that is his as the only Son of the Father'. We can be sure that his is the right way, and indeed the only way.

In his helpful reflections Father Michael Hollings invites us to take the way of the Cross. He unfolds for us the scriptures, makes sure that in our search for God we never lose sight of our neighbour, guides us in prayer, invites us always to walk with honesty, and reminds us that God understands and is always ready to forgive.

I warmly commend this book as a true companion for you on your Lenten pilgrimage.

David Konstant
Bishop in Central London

Michael Hollings has written a useful and helpful book to take people through Lent by the Way of the Cross. It has a clear shape. It is written in clear language, expressing clear ideas. And it comes from the head and the heart of one of our most experienced and compassionate of pastors. He will prove a good companion to those who want to take Lent seriously, and do it by reading his book.

Simon Phipps
Bishop of Lincoln

For many years I have worked closely with Father Michael Hollings. The quality of his life and his deep devotion to our Lord leave a deep impression on all who meet him. He is a sure guide in matters spiritual and all who read these profound meditations will be led into the Presence of the Saviour who trod the Via Dolorosa on our behalf and offers to share with us His victory over sin and death. Michael has placed us in his debt by writing this outstanding Lent book.

Kenneth G. Greet
Secretary of the Methodist Conference, 1971–1984

The Way of the Cross

'If any man will come after me, let him deny himself and take up his cross and follow me.'

This sentence comes word for word in two of the four Gospels. The only difference in Luke is that he puts in 'daily' after 'cross'. John does not use the passage at all.

The purpose of this present writing is to encourage and help you to meditate on Christ's call, to reflect upon its meaning in your individual life, to discuss it with a group or with a close friend.

We are guided by the Church to keep Lent in a different and more disciplined way than the rest of the year. Prayer, fasting and the giving of alms are all seen as useful means to steer our lives to a clearer realization of Christ's words and example. Specifically we are to enter more deeply into the passion, death and resurrection of Jesus Christ, by studying and praying over the New Testament.

One way of channelling the sharing and growth of our insight is to follow the long-standing devotion of the Stations of the Cross. This devotion is normally seen as springing from the custom of European pilgrims when they visited the Holy Land. In Jerusalem they traced as far as they could the way which led from Pilate's residence to the hill of Calvary — the traditional way along which Christ would have carried the Cross on that first Good Friday, the eve of the Passover sabbath.

They brought the story back home when they came. They wanted to preserve the memory by transferring the following of the way to their own country. Gradually it took shape, eventually containing fourteen different incidents or stations beginning with Jesus before Pontius Pilate and ending with his burial. Some of these are Gospel-based, some are not.

As these meditations became popular, they were illustrated in sculpture or painting around the walls of churches, and a mini-way was formed by moving round the church from one station to another, with hymns, led-meditations and prayers. Often during Lent this became a focal service each week, but it has also been much used by individuals taking their own time and using their own meditations and prayers.

Some years ago, following the example of the East End of London, we took the way of the cross onto the streets of Notting Hill, North

Kensington. Our object was to gather together the local congregations of the various churches in the months before Easter to pray, discuss and work on the project for ecumenical and spiritual growth. And then to take the way to people in the streets and the estates over a prolonged route, so that many who do not normally meet Church or Christ in worship might have the opportunity to stand and stare — or to share.

The introduction of this element to the meditations may enliven our minds and imaginations, so that we can enter further into the passion of Jesus, align the scenes with happenings and attitudes in our own lives, and walk through Lent as more serious followers of the Lord.

The daily sections may be used for personal reading and meditation. But is is hoped that they will also form a background for group discussion and prayer. If you have never visited a church which contains the stations of the cross, it would be worth while doing so some time during Lent. Look at each illustration as you stand before it until it sinks into you.

✝ ASH WEDNESDAY
Repentance

Have mercy on me, O God, according to thy steadfast love; according to thy abundant mercy blot out my transgressions. Wash me thoroughly from my iniquity, and cleanse me from my sin!

(Psalm 51 [50]: 1–2)

The way of the Cross began in Genesis. The original tradition which was handed on orally and then written down tells of the will of God in creation. Everything is good and pleasing to God in the way in which he has made it (Genesis 1:31). When the human beings come, as it were, at the end, the story more explicitly lays upon these creatures, male and female, the good life which will entail doing the will of God (Genesis 2:15).

Much later on, the tale was to be taken up by Jesus when he says to his disciples: 'My food is to do the will of him who sent me' (John 4:34), and then to his Father, during the prayer in the Garden of Gethsemane: 'Father, if thou art willing, remove this cup from me; nevertheless not my will, but thine, be done' (Luke 22:42).

It is good to begin our annual pilgrimage through Lent to Easter along the way of the Cross with emphasis upon the Old Testament. It helps us not to put our own lives into watertight compartments. Life should be a whole, even though coming together gradually into a unity in doing the will of God. None were more conscious of this for much of the time than the Israelites of old — personal acts of sacrifice made individually or in the name of the whole people were part of the stuff of life, laid out clearly in the Law of Moses (cp. Numbers and Deuteronomy).

Sadly, but perhaps inevitably with the human race, sacrifice and symbol easily become an empty formula — a mere ritual which is done out of duty or fear, but does not touch the heart. Again and again, the chosen people had to be called back by the patriarchs and prophets to a deeper commitment, to a more heartfelt service of the will of God.

Our Lent begins on Ash Wednesday with one such call to repentance:

**'Yet even now,' says the Lord,
'return to me with all your heart,
with fasting, with weeping and with mourning;
and rend your hearts and not your garments.'**

(Joel 2:12–13)

The most famous call to repentance came from Jonah to Nineveh:

'Yet forty days, and Nineveh shall be overthrown!' And the people of Nineveh believed God; they proclaimed a fast, and put on sackcloth, from the greatest of them to the least of them.

Then tidings reached the king of Nineveh, and he arose from his throne, removed his robe, and covered himself with sackcloth, and sat in ashes.

(Jonah 3:4–6)

Ash Wednesday for us is a day to set out on our own particular way of the Cross by making some of the preparations which will help us to understand more fully the pattern of Christ's way. During Lent we examine each step he took in terms of our own faltering steps of discipleship. The words of Jesus echo the words of Joel: 'Repent, for the kingdom of heaven is at hand' (Matthew 4:17).

We should begin with repentance, not simply the outward show of the symbolic ashes on the forehead, but the deep-down conversion of heart which both Joel and Jesus are commanding. For this, it is necessary first of all to accept the wonder of God's merciful love.

Our greatest proof of this love is the life, death and resurrection of Jesus Christ. In no clearer way can God show that love than by sending his only Son. All our meditation is to centre on Jesus. Our own sense of sinfulness and need for repentance is as it were the contrast we catch out of the corner of an eye when we see ourselves in relation to Jesus, to God. So far are we removed from God in one sense, by our very nature, it is a thing of wonder that Jesus wants to be with us. Our repentance should grow from the wonder of love in our hearts responding to the love God has for us. The reality of the love of God in Jesus is to beat upon us. He does not want us to spend all our time in anguish and guilt, but he does want our love to be real, genuine, springing from his love. This means that we must come to understand that love more in our study of Jesus, while at the same time we accept that if we open ourselves to that love we are already forgiven. He is asking nothing more than that we should now follow his steps more closely, learning the will of God as we go along with mind and heart broken open to receive his message by our repentance.

Meditation   Joel 2:13

THURSDAY AFTER ASH WEDNESDAY
Prayer

Jacob was left alone; and a man wrestled with him until the breaking of the day . . . Then he said, 'Let me go, for the day is breaking.' But Jacob said, 'I will not let you go, unless you bless me.' And he said to him, 'What is your name?' And he said, 'Jacob.' Then he said, 'Your name shall no more be called Jacob, but Israel, for you have striven with God and with men, and have prevailed.' Then Jacob asked him, 'Tell me, I pray, your name.' But he said, 'Why is it that you ask my name?' And there he blessed him. So Jacob called the name of the place Peniel, saying, 'For I have seen God face to face, and yet my life is preserved.'

(Genesis 32:24, 26–30)

The three traditional areas for working upon ourselves in the penitential season of Lent are prayer, fasting and almsgiving. Today we will look at prayer, because this should be an integral part of our life. We may be able during this season to make a greater space for God, 'waste' some more time exclusively on God in prayer. Such a space has to be made according to our individual possibility, in tune with our life. Lent is the time when we are asked to reassess how we are spending time. If the foundation for repentance is to be the love of God responded to by our love, then we must seriously weigh up the need to devote additional chunks of our day or night to the development of our relationship with God. This will only come through prayer.

Many people are not convinced of the necessity of giving God time in prayer. They say that they can pray at any time, indeed all the time. However, I know that it is very unlikely that there will be a depth growth in relationship with God, unless I am prepared to 'waste time on God'. If you are unconvinced, apply the similar though different development of a human relationship which you value. Is it not true that there is a fundamental need to be with each other if we are to grow in knowledge and love of each other? Is it not true that Jesus whom we are following along his way of the Cross spent time, and even whole nights, in prayer with his Father? (Luke 6:12). If Jesus did this, what about following? I cannot see the logic of not doing so!

Such an effort is by no means easy for us. This is why I have quoted the experience of Jacob in wrestling all night, and getting wounded in the experience — a wound he kept for life. Anyone who takes seriously the call to prayer will find that the effort of prayer, the holding on to God and oneself in prayer, the struggle and waste of time, boredom and even sense of abandonment have to be wrestled with. Prayer is a self-discipline of keeping oneself in position with one whose name we scarcely know, who does not seem willing to tell us. Yet, if we do labour away and refuse to be put off, we will indeed be blessed.

The point of centring in prayer on God to the exclusion of all else for periods of time is also questioned. Yet we will give time exclusively to one we love. We will also give time exclusively to work, to recreation, to a hundred and one things. Why should God alone have to share us all the time, rather than our being prepared to wrestle with him, or sit and enjoy him, to the exclusion of other activities? It is not as though this particular time is the sum total of expenditure on God. If we are to develop overall we must also seek to bring the presence of God into the rest of life, but this is best done from the strength of the period given to him exclusively. When we practise that, then we can more readily begin what de Caussade calls 'the sacrament of the present moment', or Brother Lawrence 'the practice of the presence of God'.

One of the ways in which we can foster this type of prayer is by growing into the habit of making short ejaculatory prayers on a regular basis, during the 'exclusive' time of prayer and also perhaps the same phrase or prayer used throughout the day and night, until it becomes a habit with us. In this way, our prayer can become habitual. Choose your own phrase, long or short. Use it often, sit and ponder on it, use it in rhythm with your breathing until it is part of you, and catch yourself repeating it as you go to sleep, in odd moments of the day. What will you choose? The choice is wide open from 'Our Father' to 'Jesus', from 'Lord have mercy on me a sinner' to 'My Lord and my God'.

Another way we will follow during Lent is meditation. This word puts some people off, because it sounds difficult or dangerous, because it is associated with some Eastern non-Christian religions. But it is a very old-established way of prayer in the Christian Church. In a way you could say that when Jesus used his parables during his lifetime, he was inviting people to meditate — 'Think of the lilies of the field' (Matthew 6), 'A man went down from Jerusalem to Jericho . . . which was the neighbour?' (Luke 10), 'A man had two sons' (Luke 15). Ever since the oral handing on and then the writing down of the revelation of God, Jews and then Christians have pondered on God, on his merciful love, his will.

All prayer is getting to know God's will, our way of the Cross daily.

Prayer   Psalm 6.

FRIDAY AFTER ASH WEDNESDAY
Fasting

He made proclamation and published through Nineveh, 'By the decree of the king and his nobles: Let neither man nor beast, herd nor flock, taste anything; let them not feed, or drink water, but let man and beast be covered with sackcloth, and let them cry mightily to God; yea, let every one turn from his evil way and from the violence which is in his hands. Who knows, God may yet repent and turn from his fierce anger, so that we perish not?'

When God saw what they did, how they turned from their evil

way, God repented of the evil which he had said he would do to them; and he did not do it.

(Jonah 3:7–10)

The second traditional area for working upon ourselves is fasting. In today's world, there are many who overeat and many who starve. There are also many who take on strict dieting for their health or for the sake of their appearance. Fasting in the sense I am using it here has literally been an age-old tradition in the religions of the world, not least in Judaism and Christianity. Here it is done as an act of penance and for spiritual health, though this may well also help the body and the mind.

The ordinary meaning of fasting is connected obviously with matters of food and drink, as we see from the very harsh measures imposed by the king of Nineveh. There are many other instances of fasting in the Old Testament, and then we come on to the period in the desert spent by John the Baptist on his diet of locusts and wild honey. Lent too reminds us of Jesus Christ's forty days and nights in the desert fasting — 'and afterwards he was hungry' (Matthew 4:2).

The Roman Catholic Church used to have very strict rules of fasting during Lent, but these have now largely been removed, leaving only one or two days for strict fasting in the year, like Ash Wednesday and Good Friday. But it is also suggested quite strongly that there should be a measure of rethinking which will lead more Christians to fast on a more regular basis, say during Lent and perhaps on the Fridays throughout the year.

Moreover, fasting can have a wider connotation, as was suggested years ago:

> Is this a Fast, to keep
>   The larder lean?
>   And clean
> From fat of veals, and sheep?
>
> Is it to quit the dish
>   Of flesh, yet still
>   To fill
> The platter high with fish?
>
> Is it to fast an hour,
>   Or ragged to go,
>   Or show
> A downcast look and sour?

No: 'tis a Fast to dole
    Thy sheaf of wheat
        And meat
    Unto the hungry soul.

It is to fast from strife
    And old debate,
        And hate;
    To circumcise thy life.

To show a heart grief-rent,
    To starve thy sin,
        Not bin;
    And that's to keep thy Lent.

            Robert Herrick (1591–1674)

Today, suggestion is made that there should indeed be fasts and 'hunger meals', with an intention of giving money saved on food and drink to the poor and needy. Often these fruits of fasting are channelled towards one of the relief organizations like Christian Aid, Oxfam, the Catholic Fund for Overseas Development, and so on. Many groups and parishes and even individuals make a special effort to support each other in their endeavours to fulfil the penitential fasting spirit of Lent for the love of God and for the benefit of people less well off.

It may need serious consideration and honesty to accept that many of us in the Western world, not least in the British Isles, eat too much, and are self-indulgent with extras (Matthew 6:16–21).

Reading   Isaiah 58:1–9.

SATURDAY AFTER ASH WEDNESDAY
Almsgiving

Jesus said to his disciples: 'Be merciful, even as your Father is merciful. Judge not, and you will not be judged; condemn not, and you will not be condemned; forgive, and you will be forgiven; give, and it will be given to you; good measure, pressed

down, shaken together, running over, will be put into your lap. For the measure you give will be the measure you get back'.

(Luke 6:36–38)

The third traditional area for working upon ourselves during Lent is in almsgiving. Some mention has already been made in reference to fasting yesterday, because the fruit of our fasting can go as a gift to the needy. These need not always be those in the less developed parts of the world. We all of us know that there can be very real hardship in our own areas — hardship which comes from sheer poverty, from unemployment, from sickness, from an accident or inability to cope. We should not always be looking away from home, but having our eyes open to immediate need in our own locality.

In the Book of Tobit there is a fine passage which helps to remind us that acts of charity which we do — almsgiving — are not confined to giving money, and if we give ourselves generously then we are exposed to dislike and even danger:

In the days of Shalmaneser I performed many acts of charity to my brethren. I would give my bread to the hungry and my clothing to the naked; and if I saw any one of my people dead and thrown out behind the wall of Nineveh, I would bury him. And if Sennacherib the king put to death any one who came fleeing from Judea, I buried them secretly. For in his anger he put many to death. When the bodies were sought by the king, they were not found. Then one of the men of Nineveh went and informed the king about me, that I was burying them; so I hid myself. When I learned that I was being searched for, to be put to death, I left home in fear. Then all my property was confiscated and nothing was left to me except my wife Anna and my son Tobias.

(Tobit 1:6–20)

I find myself getting into trouble because of trying to give money or service to people who may not seem to other people in the area worthy or worth while. But I cannot help reflecting after a battering, sometimes by friends, sometimes by critics and sometimes by the ones I am trying to help, that Jesus came for the poor and for sinners. I am pretty certain if you look round about you during this Lent, you will find people with needs. They may not seem to be very likeable, let alone lovable, but they are God's creation and loved by him as surely as you and I are loved. If they are in need they tend to be loved more by him and less by you and me.

Giving, then, is founded on giving yourself. It is often easier to give a little money to someone than to give time. We do this sort of giving in order to rid ourselves of the difficulty of having to sit and listen to a story, be sympathetic, try to help in finding lodging, offering accommodation. Is this where we get the origin of the old phrase 'as cold as charity'? If I am giving money, then I can give it resentfully or patronizingly. 'God loves a cheerful giver' (2 Corinthians 9:7).

Jesus closely aligns material giving with giving of oneself:

'If any one would sue you and take your coat, let him have your cloak as well; and if any one forces you to go one mile, go with him two miles. Give to him who begs from you, and do not refuse him who would borrow from you.'

(Matthew 5:40–42)

Such a counsel from Jesus can easily be pooh-poohed as impractical and many might say it was even bad to give, especially if you are pretty sure the money will go on drink or gambling or drugs. Well, it may be so, but here we could examine ourselves upon our attitude, because it is all too easy to hide behind common sense . . . and get away with it in our own consciences . . . but perhaps not with God (cp. Matthew 25:31–46).

Whether you are living in Notting Hill or in Liverpool, in Penzance or Perth, your neighbour is your neighbour. As we walk our pedestrian way along the way of the Cross through Lent to the resurrection, the Son of Man who gave his life to follow the will of his Father and to save us from our sins asks us to see the needy neighbour on our doorstep, in our street, behind the door of the hovel or tenement — the lonely, dying, depressed, suicidal, the alcoholic or drug addict, the thief and the mugger, the sick and the bereaved, the faithless, the unlovable.

Prayer   My song is love unknown,
My Saviour's love to me,
Love to the loveless shown,
That they might lovely be.
O who am I,
That for my sake
My Lord should take
Frail flesh and die?
Samuel Crossman (1624–83)

✝ Noah and the Rainbow Covenant of God

God said, 'This is the sign of the covenant which I make between me and you and every living creature that is with you, for all future generations: I set my bow in the cloud, and it shall be a sign of the covenant between me and the earth. When I bring clouds over the earth and the bow is seen in the clouds, I will remember my covenant which is between me and you and every living creature of all flesh; and the waters shall never again become a flood to destroy all flesh. When the bow is in the clouds, I will look upon it and remember the everlasting covenant between God and every living creature of all flesh that is upon earth.' God said to Noah, 'This is the sign of the covenant which I have established between me and all flesh that is upon the earth.'

(Genesis 9:12–17)

After the story of Adam and Eve in Genesis, with its hinting at the ultimate coming of a saviour (Genesis 3:15), the first covenant God made with his people was that with Noah. The symbol of it is the beautiful one of the rainbow. The 'bow in the sky' is such a fine expression because it comes into being through the mingling of sunlight on rainfall.

All our human life is varied. Though we can look forward with hope to a time when 'God himself will be with them; he will wipe away every tear from their eyes, and death shall be no more, neither shall there be mourning nor crying nor pain any more, for the former things have passed away' (Revelation 21:3–4). Nevertheless, at the present time, which is when we are now living in God's will, we are faced with pain and tears, the daily way of the Cross and ultimately death. Our life is a rainbow. If we have nothing but sun, we are liable to personal drought; if we have nothing but a rain of pain and loss, we may personally rot.

The state of nature — the atmosphere, world ecology — is tough in a sense, but also delicate and can be put in jeopardy. Much has been developed in more recent years in awareness of the ecological problems, especially with the rapid evolution of nuclear power and its by-products. However, interest and concern in this country are patchy. It would be well for us to consider in the light of God's covenant with all living creatures how we are taking our responsibility for the state of the world. Jesus was forthright with the Pharisees and Sadducees:

'When it is evening, you say; "It will be fair weather; for the sky is red." And in the morning, "It will be stormy today, for the sky is red and threatening." You know how to interpret the appearance of the sky, but you cannot interpret the signs of the times.'

(Matthew 16:2–3)

The bow was put in the sky as the sign of God's covenant after the chaos which had been caused in the world by disagreements between people — to be highlighted later in the story of the Tower of Babel. I wonder how blind we are to the signs of the times in our day? Lent calls us to re-adjust our materialistic and sloppy outlook, to come into line with God's covenant, and so we prepare to do this through the renewal of Baptismal promises at Easter.

Meditation   Psalm 104 [103]:5–9.

MONDAY

Jesus is condemned to death

When morning came, all the chief priests and the elders of the people took counsel against Jesus to put him to death; and they bound him and led him away and delivered him to Pilate the governor.

(Matthew 27:1–2; cp. Matthew 26:65–68)

Though the first station on the road to Calvary is generally seen as the moment when Pontius Pilate handed Jesus over to death, the reality of the condemnation began before that and within Jesus' own people, the chosen people.

If we are to understand the way which Jesus trod, then we must realize the gradual working out of his Father's will which he pondered in his early Nazareth days, at his baptism and later when driven by the Spirit into the desert.

From then onwards, he was on the forward march towards his death on the cross. His initial popularity soon brought him also jealousy and hostility. After he healed on the Sabbath, the Pharisees 'took counsel against him, how to destroy him' (Matthew 12:14); he spoke openly against the Pharisees (cp. Mark 7:1–13); he foretold the outcome (Mark 8:31–33, 9:31–32), and he set his face towards Jerusalem.

These facts should remind us that the following of God's will — for us, not less than for Christ — is going at times to be painful and distressing (cp. Matthew 10:24–25). Trying to follow Christ may lead to condemnation. Yet which of us wants that? Is it not much easier and happier to seek the quiet life and have no enemies?

Christ teaches us differently. He preaches what he has been given by his Father. As so often happens, those who start full of praise and admiration swiftly turn into critics, while those who have been critics all along continue into violent condemnation. We only have to look at the kind of campaigns which all too frequently appear in the press and the media hounding individuals.

It may be that you can think in your own life, in your neighbourhood, of someone who has been spoken about, criticized, condemned, even perhaps driven to suicide; or someone whose reputation has been ruined. Scandals there are and will be, for we are all sinners. But pointing the finger is a dangerous occupation and is particularly dangerous when the person pointing has some authority in church, state or the law.

Prejudice comes into this, and we are liable to be prejudiced whatever we may say. Prejudice is often most strong in religious circles, as it seems to have been with the chief priests and elders. This is certainly sadly true between different religions, denominations and races, and has led in the past and even the present to bloody religious conflicts, as in our near-home nightmare of Northern Ireland. On our doorstep, especially in our cities, in areas like Notting Hill, Brixton, Toxteth, Southall or Bradford there is considerable deep-seated racism. Nor is it confined to cities. Sometimes prejudice is worse where there is no racial mixture — either from ignorance or from fear.

Peter, who shared in the betrayal of Christ through fear, later had prejudice against non-Jews, but eventually came through that prejudice in a way we must all do (Acts 10:34).

It is easy to condemn the chief priests and others for sending Christ to his death. But we can talk about people, can blow hot one minute and cold another, we can neglect those in need. All this should press upon our consciences, but merely feeling guilty does not help anyone or go far. Jesus Christ would want not only the tears of Peter, but his later responses in love — 'Lord, you know everything; you know that I love you' (John 21:17).

Prayer   Sometimes they strew his way,
And his sweet praises sing;
Resounding all the day
Hosannas to their King.
Then 'Crucify!'
Is all their breath,
And for his death
They thirst and cry.

They rise, and needs will have
My dear Lord made away;
A murderer they save,
The Prince of Life they slay.
Yet cheerful he
To suffering goes,
That he his foes
From thence might free.

Samuel Crossman (1624–83)

TUESDAY

Jesus is condemned to death   JUDAS

While he was still speaking, Judas came, one of the twelve, and with him a great crowd with swords and clubs, from the chief priests and the elders of the people. Now the betrayer had given them a sign, saying, 'The one I shall kiss is the man; seize him.' And he came up to Jesus at once and said, 'Hail, Master!' And he kissed him. Jesus said to him, 'Friend, why are you here?' Then they came up and laid hands on Jesus and seized him.

(Matthew 26:47–50; cp. Matthew 27:3–5)

Another person who was involved in condemning Jesus to death was Judas. What was Judas after? Why did he do this awful thing? What can we learn from his action?

In the first place we are told a side of Judas in St John's Gospel, when Martha, Mary and Lazarus entertained Jesus to supper. Mary in a gesture of extravagant love took the costly ointment and anointed the feet of Jesus. The story goes on.

But Judas Iscariot, one of the disciples (he who was to betray him), said, 'Why was this ointment not sold for three hundred denarii and given to the poor?' This he said, not that he cared for the poor, but because he was a thief, and as he had the money box he used to take what was put into it. Jesus said, 'Let her alone, let her keep it for the day of my burial. The poor you always have with you, but you do not always have me.'

(John 12:4–8)

So Judas was a thief! Yet Jesus trusted him. I think that there was also something else very strong in Judas which also had its part to play. I think Judas really loved Jesus, but the love, like the thieving, had a selfish base. Judas wanted to possess Jesus, but Jesus was not to be possessed by anyone. He had told Peter to get behind him, because his thoughts were not God's. He could have said the same to Judas, but instead he showed the extravagant act of Mary as being more truly loving than Judas' misdirected statement. Mary's love came straight from her heart. She had been brought through much by Jesus, and she loved in a way which meant she was willing to respond, in a way which cost not less than everything. Judas on the other hand wanted his own ends, to seem to have the right ideas, to be putting forward the cause of those for whom Jesus was always speaking and working, to be more loved and respected than Mary or John or Peter. He may have really wanted Jesus to go the temporal way, with himself growing in power.

All this must be speculation, but it is easy to love in the wrong way, and when that love cracks, inability to possess can turn love to hate. Matthew gives a slightly different version, since he says the disciples were indignant (Matthew 26:8). And Matthew makes this the point at which Judas decides it is not good enough and chooses the path of betrayal rather than the way of the Cross (Matthew 26:14–16).

Where does this leave us, as we stumble along what we hope is the way of discipleship?

A great old man, Philip Neri, who lived in Rome just after the upheavals of the Reformation and became very holy, used to say towards the end of his life: 'Lord, beware of Philip! Philip may be a traitor today!' I fancy one of our difficulties in coming to follow Jesus is that, though we may confess sinfulness, we evade the issue of our betrayal of Christ. We can sigh for Judas and his eye on the ointment value and the catch of thirty pieces of silver. Do we reflect how we can tell the odd lie, cheat now and again, betray Christ with a kiss of lust rather than love?

We live in an age of withered engagements when commitments grow thin and marriages, family relationships, attachments to belief, faithfulness to difficult friendships and other bonds easily disintegrate — I hope not always in betrayal, but often too easily, and without a positive outcome and future growth.

As regards God and Jesus Christ, we are tested in Lent about what we may be doing positively. To refuse or fail to forgive, to cut a person out of one's life or to give God up because he does not seem to answer our prayers. These are betrayals.

We would not like to hear ourselves called Judas . . . but justifiably we might be.

Matthew tells us that when Judas realized what he had done to Jesus, he repented. Sadly, he may not even at that stage have realized the immensity of Jesus' merciful love . . . and hanged himself. Despair, suicide . . . yes, I expect so. But I have been involved with so many in despair, so many attempted or successful suicides, that I feel very hopeful about Judas. I know Jesus still loves him. I believe Jesus' love and mercy can extend to him as to the repentant thief.

Meditation   Psalm 37 [36]:1–9.

WEDNESDAY

Jesus is condemned to death PILATE (i)

Pilate said to him, 'So you are a king?' Jesus answered, 'You say I am a king. For this I was born, and for this I have come into the world, to bear witness to the truth. Every one who is of the truth hears my voice.' Pilate said to him, 'What is truth?'

(John 18:37–38)

At this time of violence, with so many countries occupied or controlled by foreign powers, we are in a good situation to understand the kind of problem which must have faced the Jews in the time of Christ with the Roman Occupation. Whether we look East or West, we find strings of lands suffering oppression, imprisonment of people, torture and execution.

The plight of Christ is very real today for millions of people, and we are not much more subtle than we ever were, despite United Nations, the International Court of Justice or our own supposed development of law and civilization.

Christ is a threat to the establishment of the chief priests. They in turn want to make him seem a threat to the governor, Pilate, not because they have any interest in Pilate or his position, but to make it difficult for him and to achieve their ends.

I wonder how often we play people off against each other? On the public level, it is easy to see politicians trying to undermine each other, parties often pressing minor points into major battles, scandals being blown up out of all proportion to discredit someone or some cause.

Then we come to our own local gossip, neighbours whispering, fingers pointing, poison pen letters — or just the slight over-emphasis or twist of meaning.

Christ is here with us to bear witness to the truth. If we are his followers along the way, we have to try at all times to bear witness to the truth, even when it goes against ourselves or is unpleasant. Do we always? I doubt it. Our world is riddled with innuendoes and lies, with half-truths and 'white' lies, with get-outs and cover-ups.

Lent is a good time for each of us to reflect how conscious we are of (and conscientious about) truth in our lives.

Pilate asks, 'What is truth?' Well may he ask, as may we. Even within the Christian Churches we are always arguing over truth — of the Scriptures, of who and what Christ is, of the after-life, of hell, of sin, of authority.

Pilate had not heard Jesus say, 'I am the way, and the truth, and the life' (John 14:6).

But we have heard him say that, and ask us to listen to him and follow him. Today let us reflect upon truth as we realize that the chief priests had to find false witnesses to condemn Jesus and how we ourselves who bear the name of Christian may, by doing so, bear false witness to Christ in our very way of life. Indeed, as we pray to the all merciful, all loving God, our own lack of mercy and love can show up in grim contrast.

On the other hand, it is not always easy for us to understand the truth of God's goodness in the midst of pain and disaster, death and disorder. Not everything is clear to us. We need to centre on Christ, the truth, to meditate, to listen to him.

Meditation   John 16:12–15.

Jesus is condemned to death PILATE (ii)

They cried out, 'Away with him, away with him, crucify him!' Pilate said to them, 'Shall I crucify your King?' The chief priests answered, 'We have no king but Caesar.' Then he handed him over to them to be crucified.

(John 19:15–16; cp. John 18:39–40 and 19:1–4)

There are two matters to be considered here. Firstly, the custom of releasing someone at the Passover gave Pilate a way out, but the Jews would not let him off the hook. Instead they chose a thief, Barabbas. What a choice! And yet thieves, sadly, not least in our days, are two a penny, our prisons are crowded with them, and I certainly in my time have taken things to which I was not entitled — always finding an excuse for myself, until the moment of examining my conscience afterwards. How about you? Can you say with honesty that you have never stolen or 'knocked off', or failed to return or 'winked an eye', or 'made' on the side?

We have already said that Judas was accused of being a thief — it is ironical that another thief should compete for freedom against Christ . . . and win it.

Secondly, the weak Pilate then added to the pain of Christ by torturing him, and allowing the soldiers to mock, batter and crown him. Amnesty International have highlighted the theme of torture in many, many countries of the world — torture in custody. I personally know people who have been tortured overseas, and I know some who have been beaten up in our own police stations. Today it is also true that many a thief is a mugger or uses physical violence on the victim. There is much to ponder and pray about in regard to our own contemporary attitudes, actions or acceptance.

Within the situation where I have lived and worked over the past thirty years, I have met a seemingly endless stream of men and women who have been guilty both of thieving and of violence. Jesus did not simply dismiss as irredeemable those he came across who were sinners. He forgave, brought good out of evil. As we see Jesus here in custody, we should think of the dehumanizing effect which can penetrate both staff and inmates of prisons, and the terrible effect on prisoners' families. How could things be changed? Is there a better rehabilitation system for many criminals? Is there no more that can be done both for prison officers and offenders, and especially for offenders' families?

There are ways of becoming a prison visitor, there are welfare organizations and the Prison Christian Fellowship. What could you do? In the house where I live, which is quite large and shared by a number of people, we frequently have recommended to us offenders of various ages and backgrounds who either are out on licence before being released, or are homeless on release. Happily the members of the household rally round, but life is not always sweetness and joy. We have had some bad experiences and some disasters, but I am convinced the effort is worthwhile. Despite some mockery, some bruises and many a figurative crown of thorns, good often emerges, thank God.

Prayer   Psalm 51[50]:10–13.

FRIDAY

Jesus is made to carry his Cross (i)

When they had mocked him, they stripped him of the robe, and put his own clothes on him, and led him away to crucify him.

(Matthew 27:31: cp. Mark 15:20)

There is no way we can enter the mind of Christ at this point of his agony. To have gone through the arrest, the overnight session of questioning (so often recounted in Nazi Germany, in USSR and her satellites, in the Central and Latin American police states) with the torture of scourging, buffeting and the cruel crown of thorns wedged on his head — this was enough to weaken and wrack Jesus with pain.

Yet, at the moment when the cross or what part of it he was to carry was brought to him, the immediacy of the ultimate 'cup' which he had besought his Father to remove was starkly real (Luke 22:42).

The Italian eighteenth-century saint, Alphonsus Liguori, wrote prayers and meditations for the Way of the Cross which are still used today in many churches throughout the world. His insight is to say of Jesus, 'with what great joy you did accept the Cross' . . . joy in the hard acceptance of his Father's will. For this was the way in which he would win sinful mankind to the immense love and forgiveness of God.

It may not be easy for us to go along with this, but we all probably have the experience of the relief and almost joy which can come when we have undertaken some unpleasant work which we do not really want to do, but which we are pledged to through love and duty. The task is no less onerous or distasteful, but entering it, beginning, gives a strange satisfaction. Though in no way comparable in gravity or pain, I have found over and over again that grasping the nettle of an 'impossible' task is so much less awful once I am on the way than all the anticipation and waiting. I am sure you know what I mean.

At this station, our pause for thought should be on Jesus and his utter acceptance of this 'cup' — the way of the cross and the crucifixion. And shot through our thinking should be the words of Jesus, 'Whoever does not bear his own cross and come after me, cannot be my disciple' (Luke 14:27).

The cross which *you* are to carry is yours! Essentially it is the whole of you with your plusses and minusses of being and living. Your intelligence which can help or hinder, your background, colour, family, religious faith or anything else. Whatever is immediate to you in the home, the street, work, school, in hospital — any and everywhere.

But to follow Jesus Christ in his way, we need something of that selfless dedication to his Father's will which is the object of our prayer and fasting and almsgiving during Lent.

Meditation   Isaiah 53:3–5.

SATURDAY

✝ Jesus is made to carry his Cross (ii)

So they took Jesus, and he went out, bearing his own cross, to the place called the place of a skull, which is called in Hebrew Golgotha.

(John 19:17)

In the Old Testament, at the start of God's 'love affair' with Abraham and his descendants for ever, there was a foretaste of Jesus carrying his cross;

God had told Abraham in a vision to sacrifice his beloved son Isaac upon a mountain:

And Abraham took the wood of the burnt offering, and laid it on Isaac his son; and he took in his hand the fire and the knife. So they went both of them together. And Isaac said to his father Abraham, 'My father!' And he said, 'Here am I, my son.' He said, 'Behold, the fire and the wood; but where is the lamb for a burnt offering?' Abraham said, 'God will provide himself the lamb for a burnt offering, my son.' So they went both of them together.

(Genesis 22:6–8)

You remember the end of that story, when Abraham has been taken to the limits of an act of faith, and being about to make the sacrifice of his son, finds the God-given lamb caught in a thorn bush, and so the substitution is made, and Isaac carries on the descendants of Abraham.

At this station we can recall that Old Testament scene. Now it is God's beloved Son (Mark 1:11) Jesus Christ who carries the wood of the cross of sacrifice. And this time there is to be no substitute lamb given by God, for Jesus is the Lamb of God, who takes away the sin of the world (John 1:29).

For Jesus, the fulfilment of God's promise to Abraham must have been part of his deeply imbibed learning from the Scriptures, which he was in the world to fulfil. Who knows what thoughts he was capable of at that gratingly painful stage when the heavy wood was thrust on his shoulder and scourge-striped back. Yet, he was so much in the line of the patriarchs and prophets, so steadily facing forward to do the will of his Father and complete his work, that we dare think here of the actual working out of that part of God's covenant with Abraham.

We must ponder Jesus' teaching in regard to ourselves:

And he said to all, 'If any man would come after me, let him deny himself and take up his cross daily and follow me. For whoever would save his life will lose it; and whoever loses his life for my sake, he will save it . . . For whoever is ashamed of me and of my words, of him will the Son of man be ashamed when he comes in his glory and the glory of the Father and of the holy angels.'

(Luke 9:23–26)

This teaching or prophecy is being fulfilled and is going to be completed. It is necessary then to apply it personally and reflect upon the way in which we are facing the daily carrying of the cross. We must also look at the 'scandal' of some of Christ's words of which we may be ashamed in our own lives.

Clearly, the original disciples were frightened when Jesus was arrested.

I wonder if Peter and others were also ashamed to be associated with him (Luke 22:54–62)? And I wonder where they were while he was carrying the cross along the way?

We are often ashamed, it seems, even to confess that we are followers of Christ. We can easily become shy when challenged by other people about some of our Christian belief, or about miracles. We may be ashamed when we find others bearing heavy burdens or facing inexplicable disaster or apparent unfairness from the hand of God. Sometimes, like Peter, we can deny knowledge or relationship when someone appears extreme or we want to disassociate ourselves. So it is when statements appear in newspapers or the TV which almost make us blush — we explain them away, we label people as fanatics or misguided.

This station as we set out on Christ's carrying of the wood on which he is to be crucified is a good time to ponder the word 'deny' as it touches our sensitivities, our pride in following a man 'despised . . . one from whom men hide their faces' (Isaiah 53:3).

Meditation   Psalm 42[41]:8–11.

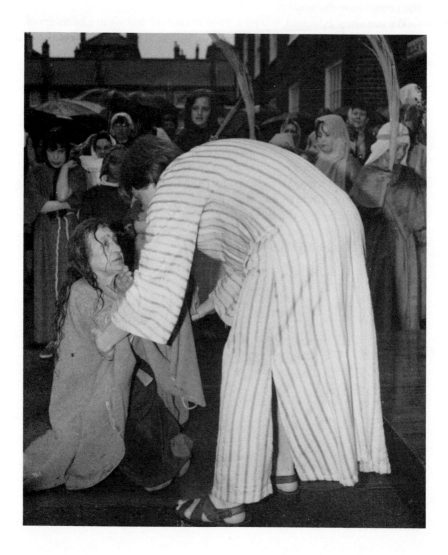

Abraham's faith and God's covenant with him

God tested Abraham, and said to him, 'Abraham!' And he said, 'Here am I.' He said, 'Take your son, your only son Isaac, whom you love, and go to the land of Moriah, and offer him there as a burnt offering upon one of the mountains of which I shall tell you.'

(Genesis 22:1–2)

'By myself I have sworn, says the Lord, because you have done this, and have not withheld your son, your only son, I will indeed bless you, and I will multiply your descendants as the stars of heaven and as the sand which is on the seashore.'

(Genesis 22:16–17)

The covenant with Noah is followed by the covenant with Abraham. This covenant is more specifically linked with the faith of Abraham. I hope you have studied the Abraham story (Genesis 11–25). If not, please do so at your leisure. It is not to be rushed. If you know the story well already, I would still advise a deeper meditative study — probably better achieved if possible with a group.

Abraham's test is a lifelong test, which covers so many aspects of life; he is called to leave his homeland and to become a pilgrim. Each of us is called, not necessarily quite like that, but to something. Firstly, are we still enough to hear the call? And secondly, if we hear, do we manage to say and do 'Yes'?

When he is on his way, it is difficult with Lot, so he generously gives him the choice, and Lot chooses the best land in the valley, leaving the higher ground to Abraham.

An ardent family man, Abraham has no child by his wife, Sarah, and has to take a concubine. Then, in his old age, he is promised a child (at which the ninety-year-old Sarah laughs!). But a child is born, Isaac, to Sarah in her old age. And as he grows, so the call again comes from God. Can you imagine it . . . all these years of waiting and hoping, then the fulfilment, and then this new call. This time it is a call which would ordinarily seem to make nonsense — that God should promise and give them a son, against all reasonable expectations (hence Sarah's laughter!), but should follow that promise and fulfilment with a demand to sacrifice that very son!

I can imagine how I would feel if this apparent changeableness in God had invaded my own life. I doubt whether I would have had the faith of Abraham. How about you? Well, in the pilgrimage of Lent towards the renewing of our own commitment or covenant, we need to ask God to strengthen our faith and our determination to pursue for another week the way of the Cross.

Prayer   Psalm 119 [118]:143–149.

MONDAY
Jesus falls for the first time (i)

For a righteous man falls seven times, and rises again; but the wicked are overthrown by calamity.

(Proverbs 24:16)

There is little written about the short journey which Jesus trod on his way to Calvary from the Praetorium. There is no mention of his falling. This and two later stations are therefore non-biblical. At the same time, their insertion into the Way of the Cross is the kind of insight which is behind much of meditation and prayer in the development of Christian thought and living.

In no sense is this insertion scholarly, nor is it part of Christian revelation. Some may wish to discard or disregard it. But as we now try stumblingly to follow the way of Jesus, I find value in realizing that Jesus was human. There has been in the past and is still present today an approach which keeps Jesus Christ so much in the realm of divinity that he scarcely touches humanity.

'The Christian faith is always a scandal to the imagination and reason of the flesh, but the particular aspect which seems most scandalous depends upon the prevailing mentality of a period or culture. Thus, to both the gnostics of the fourth century and the liberal humanists of the eighteenth, the Cross was an offense, but for different reasons. The gnostic said: "Christ was the Son of God, therefore He cannot have been physically crucified. The Crucifixion was an illusion." The liberal humanist said: "Christ was physically crucified, therefore he cannot have been the Son of God. His claim was a delusion" ' (W. H. Auden, 'The Protestant Mystics', in *Forewords and Afterwords*).

Yet Scripture tells us otherwise; we believe:

For we have not a high priest who is unable to sympathize with our weakness, but one who in every respect has been tempted as we are, yet without sinning. Let us then with confidence draw near to the throne of grace, that we may receive mercy and find grace to help in time of need.

(Hebrews 4:15–16)

It is very important to enable us to live in this world and follow Christ's steps, that we should recognize his closeness to us in all that is not sin. God did not preserve his beloved Son from the difficulties of human living. He could get tired (John 4:6), he could weep (John 11:35), and so on. Without trying to embroider our picture of Christ, because he is going ahead of us leaving an example that we should follow in his steps, it is only reasonable to believe that he does not set us an impossible task (1 Corinthians 10:13).

I suggest, then, that we look at this first fall as an insight which is truly helpful to us as we stumble after Christ. One can say that it is typical of him that he should go with us on the way, and that the 'fall' of the righteous man seven times is important to us as a realization of our own weakness, and of Christ's understanding, care and love for us. But I think too that when we see ourselves in the light of our personal faults and failures and falls, we should recall that the righteous man 'rises again'.

The Lord asks us to take up the cross *daily*. This may or may not be after a fall, and the effort or the attempt to get up and go on is always necessary for us . . . even when we fall again or do not succeed.

Prayer   Psalm 74[73]:18–23.

TUESDAY

Jesus falls for the first time (ii)

Do nothing without deliberation; and when you have acted, do not regret it. Do not go on a path full of hazards, and do not

stumble over stony ground. Do not be over confident on a smooth way, and give good heed to your paths. Guard yourself in every act, for this is the keeping of the commandments.

(Ecclesiasticus [Sirach] 32:19–23)

Many of the admonitions in the Old Testament Wisdom books are seeking perfection. We should aim high, reach for the stars. At the same time we need to keep our feet on the ground. The way of the Cross, on which Jesus leads us, is a way of life. Human beings are subject to falling, to stumbling, to doing the less good thing — or perhaps to doing the good thing not very well!

Jesus' life as it unfolds his teaching urges us to higher and better things, to the avoidance of sin, indeed to 'be perfect, as your heavenly Father is perfect' (Matthew 5:48).

The way of perfection is a path along which we plod. Our only existence is *now*. What we will be in the future is not revealed to us. We do not even know what perfection is for us now, except that we try *now* to live out what seems to be God's will for us at the present time.

Therefore, in a sense, God leaves us to get on with life, without interfering with us. When we slip and fall, he is there. Yet for us at the time, it may seem he is not there at all! One of the lessons as we see him stumbling his way to Calvary is that even in his case, God does not intervene — he is weak, and he falls. Satan reminded him:

' "He will give his angels charge of you," and
"On their hands they will bear you up,
Lest you strike your foot against a stone." '

(Matthew 4:6; cp. Psalm 91[90])

But that kind of help he rejected, for there was nothing sinful in his falling.

Should we not, then, look at our own physical weakness? When we are young and comparatively weak, we can get frustrated because we cannot pull this or push that. When we get older, we find it more difficult, because we have in the past been able to do this or that, and now we no longer have the strength . . . quite humiliating! But if for one reason or another we are physically weak, through sickness or ageing, let us accept this and know our limitations, and not fret about them. This may give us a greater opportunity to relax and reflect.

One thing we should not do is get oppressed or depressed at our weakness. To get up and go on shows a moral strength in itself, though we may not feel it.

The old saying we have had in this country is very appropriate: If at first you don't succeed, try, try, try again.

In falling, we may get very introverted, seeing ourselves as always the ones who fall. But it is a loving and supportive action on our part to accept the fact that others fall. Knowing that, 'there but for the grace of God go I', we can have more sympathy and give more moral uplift to the person who has stumbled, because we know the experience, and also because we have ourselves experienced forgiveness and the hand of the Lord helping us to our feet.

Prayer Psalm 57 [56]:1–2.

WEDNESDAY

Jesus meets his mother

(i)

The Lord God said unto the serpent . . .
'I will put enmity between you and the woman,
and between your seed and her seed;
he shall bruise your head,
and you shall bruise his heel.'

(Genesis 3:14–15)

This is another station of which there is nothing in the Gospel narrative. It is not surprising really, when we consider how little is said about Mary at any point in the story, apart from the infancy narratives. We are told of her being unable to get near Jesus during his public ministry (Mark 3:31–33), and we will hear later of her at the foot of the cross (John 19:25–27).

But this station gives us a chance which is important. We can pause for a moment and reflect upon Mary and upon motherhood, and upon the course of the working out of God's plan. I have quoted Genesis today, because a very ancient tradition has linked 'the woman' with Mary and the offspring with Jesus Christ, Son of God. The quoted passage has been seen as God's first intimation that there will be a redeemer. In the Old Testament, there is no mention or prophecy until Isaiah:

'Behold, a young woman shall conceive and bear a son, and shall

call his name Immanuel. He shall eat curds and honey when he knows how to refuse the evil and choose the good.'

(Isaiah 7:14–15)

The importance of Mary is in her motherhood, according to revelation decreed for her by God. In other words, we can reflect again at this point upon the main work of our lives, which is to seek the will of God and then do it. We have the story of Mary being told about her motherhood, querying it as any woman would do; then, when satisfied in faith that the message was genuine, saying simply but profoundly: 'Behold, I am the handmaid of the Lord; let it be to me according to your word' (Luke 1:38).

At a later stage what might at first seem to be almost a snub to the speaker and by implication to Mary, can be seen as an underlining authentic acceptance and living out of her promise (Luke 11:27–28).

This station helps us ponder the meeting of Mary and Jesus, mother and son, in such a situation. Whatever else we may say or think about Mary, it is clear from her later place near the cross that she had not run away — she was still with her son, still intent on completing the work of motherhood which God had given her.

For us, the lesson of faithfulness is one which needs restressing in our time, owing to the problems of modern society which are causing so much breakdown in marriage, so much chaos in relationships, sometimes between mother and child.

Meditation   Isaiah 49:15.

THURSDAY

Jesus meets his mother

(ii)

**'As one whom his mother comforts,
so I will comfort you;
you shall be comforted in Jerusalem.'**

(Isaiah 66:13)

Living at various times in different parts of England, Scotland and Wales, to say nothing of Ireland, I have been fascinated and moved to watch the underlying nature of motherhood while at the same time noting that there are quite a few subtle differences. These are not only from one mother to another, from one family to another. They are also differences inherited or brought about by varying cultural backgrounds.

This is a very sensitive area and one I do not mean to discuss in any way which could be construed as racist. There are reasons for attitudes being varied, for methods of approach to marriage and to child education having a wide spectrum. And indeed even one generation of mothers can differ from another.

But the underlying principle is love. Without love, a mother is no mother.

The point stressed in this meeting of Jesus and his mother is that she was *there*. I do not know how you are placed as you read this — female or male, old or young, married or single, with children or without. I was very blessed in my mother, who was kind and firm, worked for us when we were young, allowed us to grow our wings and fly from home, yet remained there, always loving and caring. I think if one of us had ended in court or been condemned to death, she would have been there, hating it all, hating anything we had done wrong, but still loving us completely, forgiving anything needing to be forgiven and ready to stand by us.

This is the idea I would have of Mary and the ideal I would want all mothers, fathers, brothers, sisters, cousins and friends to foster in themselves as the foundation for all human beings . . . faithfulness and love.

I confess that wandering the streets of London and other places, not every mother, father or friend comes anywhere near the ideal. Which of us does? But there is a lot of love, support and comfort given. There are really heroic families battling against alcohol, breakdown, depression, crime, debt, and so on. Among the saddest things are visits to hospitals and to prisons. Both have tremendous queues of visitors. It is not easy to visit someone who is dear and dying, perhaps day after day, week after week. It is shaming to visit a relative or friend in prison . . . I can tell you because apart from others, I have been visiting two men for some twelve years now.

God's word quoted from Isaiah refers immediately to the people of Israel. We can also take it to have reference to God's care for his Son, which may well have led Mary, follower of God's will, on to the streets of Jerusalem, there to comfort her son Jesus. And we can take it as a promise to ourselves of God's everlasting love (Jeremiah 31:3).

It is for us to assure our positive development of that love which is within us all, so that we are faithful in our homes and on our streets and try our best to be loving, even when we come face-to-face with our personal horror.

Consideration 'I was able to understand something of the compassion of our Lady St Mary. She and Christ were so one in their love that the greatness of her love caused the greatness of her suffering. In this I found an example of that instinctive love that creation has to him — and which develops by grace. This sort of love was most fully and supremely shown in his dear Mother. Just because she loved him more than did anyone else, so much the more did her sufferings transcend theirs. The higher, and greater, and sweeter our love, so much deeper will be our sorrow when we see the body of our beloved suffer.'

(Julian of Norwich, *Revelations of Divine Love*, ch. 18)

FRIDAY
Jesus meets his mother

IV

(iii)

His mother said to him, 'Son, why have you treated us so? Behold, your father and I have been looking for you anxiously.' And he said to them, 'How is it that you sought me? Did you not know that I must be in my Father's house?' And they did not understand the saying which he spoke to them. And he went down with them and came to Nazareth, and was obedient to them; and his mother kept all these things in her heart.

(Luke 2:48–51)

For Mary the way of the Cross, though she did not know it as such, began when she said her 'Yes' to God. Similarly, our way of the Cross has begun at some point or must begin at some point. Baptism, if we were baptized in infancy, has to be accepted individually at a later stage. An alternative is conversion.

I personally was baptized as an infant, gave up in my teens and then had a conversion. Since then, I have said 'Yes' to God on innumerable occasions. But I realize I have also said 'No' to God. My 'Yes' has been imperfect. How about yours, if you have made it? If you have not, would this Lent be a time to meet Jesus and say 'Yes' to him, even in such difficult circumstances as Mary had when she met him on the way to his death?

She had met him so much before. As his mother, she was 'home' all the time until he left her, and home for his own personal following of his Father, his own 'Yes' to God.

Mary had to 'keep all these words in her heart' from the annunciation by the angel, through all that followed in the hidden life. She then had to watch him 'destroying' himself as he preached, healed and drew anger and hatred from the scribes, Pharisees and chief priests.

All the time, Mary had to be faithful to God and to Jesus. It can't have been easy!

How many mothers, and fathers also, find it intensely difficult to go along with what their sons and daughters wish to do? Wish to be!

Here is something worth thinking about. Look into the Scripture, look at the quality of God's love! He is always faithful, and though he is often pictured as 'angry', he always relents. There is no better picture of God's love than that given by Jesus in the story of the prodigal son . . . the father ever on the watch for the errant son; after allowing the freedom to go his own way, he is there waiting in love and forgiveness for his return. Well may people speak of God as mother as well as father, for he is both in the truest sense because he is love.

But we know that we do not always understand love. It must have been very difficult for Mary to be left when Jesus chose all the disciples from among the men and spent so much of his time with them. Yet she remained faithful to him, still needing to keep all these things in her heart.

This age is no easy age to be a parent. The mixture of firmness and approachability, of love and yet discipline, of giving freedom yet keeping a standard — all these attitudes are hard to cultivate amid the ordinary and extraordinary pressures and stresses.

We can take courage from the courage of Mary, from the example of the patience of God, and from the resolution of Jesus following the way of his Father's will even under the weight of the cross.

Meditation   Luke 2:41–52.

SATURDAY

Jesus meets his mother

(iv)

'And I will make for you a covenant on that day with the beasts of the field, the birds of the air, and the creeping things on the ground; and I will abolish the bow, the sword, and war from the land; and I will make you lie down in safety. And . . . I will betroth you to me in righteousness and in justice, in steadfast love and in mercy. I will betroth you to me in faithfulness; and you shall know the Lord.'

(Hosea 2:18–20)

Hosea, the prophet, had a wife who was a harlot. There was much sorrow and distress, but the prophecy was that all should come right, as illustrated by his own life.

The way of the Cross for each one of us is our own life:

'You cannot escape it, whithersoever you run. For wheresoever you go you carry yourself with you, and shall always find yourself. Turn upwards or turn downwards, turn inwards or turn outwards; everywhere, you shall find the cross.'

(Thomas à Kempis, *Of the Imitation of Christ*, ii.12)

If this applies to us, it applied also to Mary, the Mother of Jesus. And so it was that she found herself and Jesus each carrying their cross on that Friday before the Passover. For us the symbolism of the Passover is not so great. Although we have it as the origin of the paschal lamb, it was much more vivid to the Jew of Jesus' day (read Exodus 12:5–7 and 11).

The people of Israel were about to go out on their own pilgrimage, their own way of the Cross, which was to take them for forty years' journeying through the desert towards the promised land. For many of them, Moses being one, that land was not to be reached in this life. But they journeyed on in a mingling of hope and despair, of faithfulness and idolatry — a more than usually tough, but a typical pattern of the pilgrimage of mankind.

For Jesus and Mary, the pilgrimage was not so wandering, as it was set inexorably in God's will. But the way is not always so plain. An understanding of it, illustrated from Bunyan, is laid out by a recent author: speaking of Bunyan's pilgrim, he writes that he 'feels continually the problem of taking directions and finding his way. The entire story has Christian repeatedly renewing a mysterious impulse which caused him at the outset to leave his wife and children to head off in bewilderment, except concerning the single point that an interior light, which he could not command, was to be his guide. Bunyan thus draws attention to the mystery within: Christian follows one highly particular course to Jerusalem, and his adventures are less important for the progress they suggest along a pre-existent route which all men can follow, than for their insistence on the continuing mystery of interior illumination by which God leads him (and consequently, each one of us) through any diversity of circumstances' (Patrick Grant, *The Literature of Mysticism in the Western Tradition*).

So for each of us, as for Jesus on his way to Jerusalem and the Cross, or Mary giving birth and then following her son along the way, there is an inner light. But this can be obscured, we can feel lost, the light can seem to go out, we grope. Yet the word remains: 'Follow me'.

Prayer   Lead, kindly Light, amid the encircling gloom,
            Lead thou me on;
        The night is dark, and I am far from home;
            Lead thou me on.
        Keep thou my feet; I do not ask to see
        The distant scene; one step enough for me.

        I was not ever thus, nor prayed that thou
            Shouldst lead me on;
        I loved to choose and see my path; but now
            Lead thou me on.
        I loved the garish day, and, spite of fears,
        Pride ruled my will: remember not past years.
                        John Henry Newman (1801–1890)

The Ten Commandments

'The LORD our God is one LORD; and you shall love the LORD your God with all your heart, and with all your soul, and with all your might. And these words which I command you this day shall be upon your heart; and you shall teach them diligently to your children, and shall talk of them when you sit in your house, and when you walk by the way, and when you lie down, and when you rise.'

(Deuteronomy 6:4–7)

'You shall not take vengeance or bear any grudge against the sons of your own people, but you shall love your neighbour as yourself.'

(Leviticus 19:18)

'On these two commandments depend all the law and the prophets.'

(Matthew 22:40)

The development of the covenant gradually became more formalized. This was especially so in the giving of the commandments of the Law to Moses — the ten commandments (Exodus 20:1–17). The minutiae of detail worked out over the years for the fulfilment of the Law became a heavy burden on the ordinary person, and a weapon in the hands of the chief priests.

I often tell how a lady, a parent, came one day to tell me her small child was at a very bad Catholic school. I asked why it was bad. She said it did not teach the Catholic Faith. So I asked what it did not teach. She replied that it didn't teach the ten commandments. I asked what it did teach and she replied it was something very odd about loving God and your neighbour!

Everything is summed up in loving God, oneself and other people. But the way that this is carried out can be elaborated into ten or ten times ten commandments, laws, bye-laws and admonitions. Not unnaturally, as the Church has gone on through the centuries into different lands and different peoples, different customs and different cultures. Sometimes laws have been simplified in an effort at reform; sometimes they have just become more complicated.

So, where do we stand? If we want to follow the will of God, if we want to take up our cross each day, then we must be prepared for the pattern of living which the Lord is setting before us. Our effort and our difficulty may well be that we are to follow the commandments, but this does not mean that we get into scrupulous details, nor does it mean that we ride roughshod over all provisions.

Only by prayer, meditation and study of the law of God, by studying God himself through Jesus Christ, are we going to come to some kind of clarity about the commandments, the universal law of God's love.

This is worth a genuine, deep study, and a prayerful one, on the Lenten way of the Cross, leading to renewal of faith and commitment.

Meditation Psalm 119 [118]:1–3.

MONDAY
Simon of Cyrene is made to help Jesus (i)

As they went out, they came upon a man of Cyrene, Simon by name; this man they compelled to carry his cross.

(Matthew 27:32)

Almost as a support for the insight that Jesus fell on his way, as he gradually became weaker from exhaustion, pain and loss of blood, we have the statement in three evangelists that the soldiers found it necessary to compel an ordinary man in the crowd to help carry the cross.

One of the Christian notes about the saving work of Christ in the incarnation is that he enlists the aid of his followers to carry on the work which he has set out to do for his Father.

The theological proposition is that God works through secondary causes. This simply means that he is behind and through and in his creation, but he is not all the time interfering in the working out of his overall plan for that creation. We do not really know how much is involved in the day-by-day working of nature in the universe, but clearly whole patterns of life and culture can be changed by natural disasters. The story of the flood (Genesis 6–8) is a biblical example of this, and more and more is being discovered about the movement of land masses, the origins of earthquakes and volcanic eruptions and so forth.

But the main secondary cause which God uses in the day-by-day development of mankind is the human being, who not only has much power and influence among fellow men and women, but can also become more and more able both to exploit or conserve the world — or to destroy it totally through nuclear warfare.

Abraham, Moses and David made immense differences in the destiny of the chosen people (cp. Genesis to 1 Kings). After that the many prophets also had a profound effect. But alongside these, there were men and women who were not the followers of the one God. They too made their contribution. So it is to the present day, and will be till the end of human existence (Matthew 28:18–20).

Involved in Christ's incarnation were John the Baptist, Joseph and Mary, the apostles, high priests, Judas, Pilate, and Simon of Cyrene.

Each of us is created by God to fulfil his purpose. But we can do as we please, and refuse to serve him if we like. Sometimes, however, a person seems to be seized by God. For instance, Jeremiah:

**'Before I formed you in the womb I knew you,
and before you were born I consecrated you;
I appointed you a prophet to the nations.'**

Then I said, 'Ah, Lord GOD! Behold, I do not know how to speak, for I am only a youth.' But the LORD said to me,

**'Do not say, "I am only a youth";
for to all to whom I send you you shall go,
and whatever I command you you shall speak.'**

(Jeremiah 1:5–7)

Another very sharp example is Saul called on the road to Damascus (Acts 9:1–9).

Simon is in this tradition, though to us more clearly seen and more physically involved. Let it give us an incentive to ask ourselves how Jesus may be asking us to share in his sufferings and also in his mission of fulfilling God's will in this world.

Meditation   Psalm 25 [24]:8–10.

TUESDAY

Simon of Cyrene is made to help Jesus (ii)

And they compelled a passer-by, Simon of Cyrene, who was coming in from the country, the father of Alexander and Rufus, to carry his cross.

(Mark 15:21)

The Old Testament is full of stories of people who have been touched by God and joined in his service or refused to do so. Most of these stories are complete. In the New Testament, I find myself wanting to know the end of the story. What, for instance, happened to the woman Jesus spoke to at the well at Samaria? She so plainly went to serve the Lord by spreading his name to her township (John 4:7–42). But after that? Did she hear that Jesus had been crucified? Did she and her several husbands and townsfolk get to know of the resurrection? Or the widow and her resurrected son of Nain? Did he outlive her? Did his new life *change* his way of life (Luke 7:11–15)? Or did the centurion whose faith Jesus had found 'not even in Israel' (Luke 7:9) — where was he at the time of the way of the Cross? Had he been posted back to Rome as one who was being 'corrupted by mad preachers', or what? There must be some you would like to know about also, and if it still interests us, perhaps it will be part of the glory of heaven that we shall know!

But with Simon we have a testimony that the outcome was for him to become a Christian, at least that would be the assumption, since Mark refers to his sons Alexander and Rufus, and so they were presumably known to those for whom Mark was writing.

It would still be interesting to know whether Jesus said anything to Simon, or whether he met Mary by the cross, or John. Did he wait while Christ died on the cross, did he perhaps go back with the disciples to the place where they stayed over the Sabbath, and so join in the dismay — and then joy of the news 'He is risen'? We do not know, but remember that Christ's touch comes often unexpectedly.

This understanding helps us to hope when someone we love drops God, or someone we love refuses to come near belief. In my experience such extraordinary, wonderful and unexpected happenings occur, that I am never surprised now when someone comes, as it were, out of the blue and wants to 'see Jesus' (John 12:21).

Some time ago, a man who had been unable to believe at all was asked by his wife to come on a Good Friday procession of witness. He absolutely refused. But something happened during the Easter weekend. On Easter Monday, his wife came into my room and said to me I must come into the church as her husband was there. I came. He was kneeling in the church saying over and over again: 'I want Jesus! I want Jesus!'

As you continue to take up your cross and follow Jesus, be prepared both for darkness and frustration — and for miracles of grace.

Prayer   Psalm 136 [135]:3–5.

WEDNESDAY

Simon of Cyrene is made to help Jesus (iii)

A brother helped is like a strong city,
but quarrelling is like the bars of a castle.   (Proverbs 18:19)

It is human to come together to form families, tribes and communities, which then live and work with each other for the personal and common benefit.

As we see Simon trudging behind Jesus sharing the burden of his cross we can realize that though he is partaking in a terrible action — assisting in the eventual death of Jesus on the cross they are carrying — he is also playing his part in the act of redemption. He is immediately and physically helping with the load. He also gains faith from doing so, and afterwards, no doubt, his sons stress to the young Christian community their father's part in this great drama which led up the hill to death, but beyond the hill to resurrection and new life.

In the Christian Church in the past ten years or so, there has been a renewed interest in and experimentation with the establishment and building of differing types of community living. Older religious communities have often shrunk, or deliberately formed themselves into smaller communities. At the same time, especially in Latin America, there has been a huge growth in 'basic communities' — groups set up which do not necessarily share accommodation, but are linked in study, work and worship, many times without a priest, and at the ground roots of local society. This is in the Church.

But also in society, there is an increasing need for the sense of urgency in order to get to grips with the fragmenting of society and the breakdown of relationships on a large scale.

The story of the early Church in the Acts of the Apostles gives an indication of the way in which, immediately after the ascension of Jesus Christ, the believers banded together:

And all who believed were together and had all things in common; and they sold their possessions and goods and distributed them to all, as any had need. And day by day, attending the temple together and breaking bread in their homes, they partook of food with glad and generous hearts, praising God and having favour with all the people . . .

(Acts 2:44–47)

Perhaps it was into such grouping that Simon of Cyrene came, and perhaps we should be looking today to our own structuring. It is clear that the size and often impersonal atmosphere of a parochial setting is not right to catch the mood, the interest and the involvement of the majority even of Christians. It is worth casting round and discussing among parish communities and local neighbours how best we can set about helping each other in living the faith, and helping those who have no faith and are at present untouched.

One way which we have found helpful has been the one illustrated through this book — people coming together to prepare, make costumes for and then put on an enactment of the way of the Cross through the streets of the district. Worked on for over a year, it bound us together a lot. There are many other ecumenical groupings which help an area, wider than an individual church. Where there are people from various ethnic backgrounds it is a purposeful work to initiate ways of cross-fertilizing.

Meditation Acts 10:34–43.

✝ VI Veronica wipes the face of Jesus (i)

Even if our gospel is veiled, it is veiled only to those who are perishing. In their case the god of this world has blinded the minds of the unbelievers, to keep them from seeing the light of the gospel of the glory of Christ, who is the likeness of God. For what we preach is not ourselves, but Jesus Christ as Lord, with ourselves as your servants for Jesus' sake. For it is the God who said, 'Let light shine out of darkness,' who has shone in our hearts to give the light of the knowledge of the glory of God in the face of Christ.

(2 Corinthians 4:3–6)

Here we have another 'invented' station, not mentioned in the Bible. Why then should it be there, and how can we connect such an incident with the message of the gospel? The Fourth Gospel, the Gospel of John, whether written by him, his 'school' or someone else, ends as we have it now with the verse:

But there are also many other things which Jesus did; were every one of them to be written, I suppose that the world itself could not contain the books that would be written.

(John 21:25)

This does not mean that anyone has a licence to invent anything and say it is authentic. The story of Veronica is not authentic in that it is not part of the Bible. In a late version of the apocryphal work the *Acts of Pilate* the name Veronica is attributed to the woman who suffered from an issue of blood (Matthew 9:20–22). The present form applying the name to a woman of Jerusalem may have originated in France and about the fourteenth century. Here the legend was that she offered her headcloth to wipe the face of Jesus from the bloody sweat which covered it, and when she looked at it she saw an imprint of his features on the cloth. Sometimes the name (which is Latin, meaning 'true image') is given to the cloth, sometimes to the woman herself. In the Middle Ages there was great devotion, with more than one place in Italy claiming the original headcloth. Such is the story.

I have already quoted Isaiah 53:2. I think this is a balancing vision to that — because I believe that the glory of Jesus Christ is not simply a post-resurrection glory, but one which shines through him as he walked in

Palestine so long ago, when the interior light in him shone forth into the hearts of others.

One of the modern holy women of France, Thérèse of Lisieux, had as her name in religion 'of the Child Jesus and the Holy Face'. During her life as a Carmelite sister, she wrote that she had come to see in the battered and bloodied face of Jesus the merciful love of God.

This is why I would want you to look at the face of Jesus Christ and to ask for the kind of enlightenment which Paul speaks of in the passage I have quoted at the beginning of this day. I can in a small way sense and know the horror of what was done to Jesus and was continuing to be done to him. But the wonder of it is that this aspect is the face of love. Love and suffering go hand in hand, and we must recognize it, but his promise is there to give us a lift through what might otherwise seem horrific and insupportable (Matthew 11:28–30).

Meditation   Isaiah 53:10–12.

FRIDAY
Veronica wipes the face of Jesus (ii)

Who shall ascend the hill of the LORD?
And who shall stand in his holy place?
He who has clean hands and a pure heart,
who does not lift up his soul to what is false,
and does not swear deceitfully.
He will receive blessing from the LORD,
and vindication from the God of his salvation.
Such is the generation of those who seek him,
who seek the face of the God of Jacob.

(Psalm 24 [23]:3–6)

If the name Veronica is taken as the name of the woman of Jerusalem who wiped the face of Jesus on his way to Calvary, then we can take the meaning — true image — and refer it to her and to her representation of women.

On the whole, women do not seem to have much of a look in in the Bible.

But that, of course, is partly to do with the nature of the Judaic society of the time.

However, there were some women highlighted, though sometimes in doubtful situations. Rebekah, wife of Isaac, changed the whole course of the history of the descendants of Abraham to whom the promise had been given, by substituting her beloved son Jacob for her less loved son Esau (Genesis 27 and onwards). One of the apocryphal books tells the story of Judith, which again is a bit dubious, but shows the courage and purpose of a loyal Jewess. Ruth is rather a beautiful story of kindness and love. Esther again was a fearless defender of her people, and went into great danger for them. She was the one who instituted a fast asking God's favour when the safety of the Jewish people was threatened (Esther 4:16).

More interestingly, we have various encounters which Jesus himself has with women and his obvious care and assurance of them. His approach to the Samaritan woman at the well is a classic example — starting from where she was, and asking something of her, and then gradually working through to a theological and then moral discussion, until the moment comes when the woman is ready to become an apostle . . . she goes to her township and spreads the good news of Jesus Christ (John 4). At the other end of the Gospel, at the resurrection, Jesus makes Mary Magdalen the first bearer of the news of his rising from the dead (John 20:17–18).

As Veronica is the 'true image', we might ask ourselves whether the Church has been in the past, and is in the present, rightly open to women and their role in the Church and in the world? The Church has the responsibility to the 'true image' of God, of Jesus Christ and of God's creation to make sure that women share equality with men. There is a long way to go in this, and a great deal of prejudice to overcome, but that is all the more reason for us to press on in our local parishes and in the Church as a whole. It is easier to get things going at local level that to wait for solemn pronouncements. There are so many ways theoretically open for women in the Church. It is for all of us to try to make certain that in our neighbourhood there is an equality of opportunity not only in the Church, but in every walk of life.

Meditation   2 Corinthians 3:12–18.

SATURDAY

✝

Ⅵ

Veronica wipes the face of Jesus (iii)

He will destroy on this mountain the covering that is cast over all peoples, the veil that is spread over all nations. He will swallow up death for ever, and the Lord GOD will wipe away tears from all faces, and the reproach of his people he will take away from all the earth; for the LORD has spoken.

(Isaiah 25:7–8)

As Jesus is on the way to that death which the Lord 'will swallow up for ever', a person anticipates the work of God. In her one action for the pilgrim Jesus, she wipes away tears, sweat and blood from his face. Her generous expression of love and compassion takes away the reproach from the people who are 'going along' with the authorities and not giving support to Jesus. Twice when we have done our Way of the Cross through the streets of Notting Hill, the scene of Veronica wiping the face of Jesus has been doubly moving because of the scenery of this London of ours; it was not so much sweat to be wiped from the brow of the Christ-figure, but rain which poured down torrentially, making our local scene more real. In Jerusalem, on that awful day, it may have been very hot, in addition to all the other local hazards — flies, mosquitoes, smells, garbage on the way, stinking drains, crowds' hostility — the rest. Here we often suffer different hazards — cold, rain, darkness, indifference.

A central purpose of the life of Jesus is to focus us onto the reality of living where, when and how we are. Incarnation is here and now. The way of the Cross is here and now. The crucifixion is here and now, for me in London, Bayswater/Notting Hill; for you wherever you are.

Too easily we can put everything about the way of the Cross into an historical past, where we are voyeurs of the tragic scene. NO! Jesus lived there and then. He worked his way out in awful realism and reality. But he wants us to work out our own living Way of the Cross in stark realism and reality . . . NOW, HERE!

Veronica symbolizes for us the true reaction. She ignored all hostility, sneering, filth of word of mouth, dishonour in the eyes of her neighbours. She simply did her work of love and compassion.

As we try during this Lent to follow the way of the Cross, let us try to bring it down to our own dimension in Notting Hill, Brixton, Bradford, Penzance, the Shetlands, or Derry. If Christ is dying in Notting Hill and every other place in the world, then *you and I* 'are Christ' dying in these places. We are his body. He lives in us, he witnesses through us. If someone says that the Church is cold, it is not Christ who is cold, but you and I who express no caring.

Female or male, it is you and I who are at this time expected by Jesus to be the 'Veronicas', the true images of what it is to be human and to be imbued with the love of God and the thirst for souls which Jesus expresses on his way to the Cross.

Prayer   Psalm 116 [115]:7–9.

Jerusalem our Mother. Mother's Day

'Rejoice with Jerusalem, and be glad for her,
all you who love her;
rejoice with her in joy,
all you who mourn over her;
that you may suck and be satisfied
with her consoling breasts;
that you may drink deeply with delight
from the abundance of her glory.'

(Isaiah 66:10–11)

Mother's Day originated at this date from the opening verse of the Eucharist which is quoted above. The symbol of the Mother has always been very strong. Roman Catholics for instance refer to *'Holy Mother Church'*. The pilgrimage of Jesus Christ was towards Jerusalem, and came to a climax on the road to Calvary. Symbolically, God is asking each of us to take up this journey, to set our faces towards Jerusalem (cp. Luke 9:51). During Lent we endeavour to put one foot in front of the other on the path of prayer, fasting and almsgiving. We may well stumble, but that is to be our continous way.

Now, going to Jerusalem our 'mother' does not mean that we are thinking about Baptism in the way Nicodemus seemed to think (John 3:3–5).

Jesus answered him, 'Truly, truly, I say to you, unless one is born anew, he cannot see the Kingdom of God.' Nicodemus said to him, 'How can a man be born when he is old? Can he enter a second time into his mother's womb and be born?' Jesus answered, 'Truly, truly, I say to you, unless one is born of water and the Spirit, he cannot enter the kingdom of God.'

We are not trying to get back into the womb, to hide, to seek security. Rather, our 'mother' Jerusalem is offering us this rebirth by water and the Holy Spirit which may also be sometimes a rebirth by blood, in the case of a martyr.

However, this symbol of mother gives us a good opportunity and incentive to think about our origins and our allegiances. As one who disowned my original Baptism into the family of Jesus Christ, I can assure you that the process of re-assessment and re-discovery is well worth while. I have never regretted the re-kindling of faith in me. Since then, I have often wavered and doubted, but each time, partly from the solid basis of rediscovered good and partly from the attraction of a combination of security and mystery, I have found myself making yet another act of faith, and carrying on along the way.

We have a chance today to be very simple, even a little sentimental, and to thank and praise God not only for his incorporation of ourselves into his body, but also to thank God for the most wonderful gift in life . . . the gift of our mothers. May it be a happy day for them. May it be a day we can give a two-fold thanks . . . to God our Father and our human mother.

Meditation   Psalm 87 [86]:1–3, 5, 7.

MONDAY
Jesus falls a second time
VII

(i)

We beseech you on behalf of Christ, be reconciled to God. For our sake he made him to be sin who knew no sin, so that in him we might become the righteousness of God.

(2 Corinthians 5:20–21)

Like us in all things but sin, Jesus had to bear the weight of the human body. He was not 'Superman'. He was man! The way of the Cross, if the way which is traditional today is truly the one he had to tread, was quite short. But for a person in the condition that Christ must have been in by that time, every step must have seemed a mile.

And here we meditate on a second fall. The fall itself perhaps jarred him, with the cross coming down on top of his already bleeding and battered body.

The meditation we do is not just to underline the horror of the scene and the suffering of Jesus. These are real indeed, but his lesson is wider and deeper. After all, given TV, we are all exposed to a seemingly endless series of horror stories, with the factual ones often being more gruesome and horrific than the imaginative creation of the fiction writer!

This fall highlights the common humanity which Jesus has with each one of us. We do not find it easy — many of us, that is — to develop in ourselves or allow to develop the sense of close brotherhood which Jesus has with us. Without belittling Christ, we are asked to grasp the wonder of this condescension of God that his Son should wear and bear our humanity. But even when I use the word 'condescension', I get worried because in our day and age, such a word smacks of paternalism.

We have developed a great deal over the centuries. We have discovered through psychology many things about the human person we did not know before so explicitly — though frequently the wisdom seems to have been shining through revelation and the practice of the Church, even when the 'proper' psychological terms had not been defined! Unfortunately, it sometimes seems that whatever action is taken, a psychological term can be attached to it which appears to undermine the value or credibility of what is being done.

A father acts as a father. God 'acts' as God. And he sets the pattern for us. As St Paul wrote:

I bow my knees before the Father, from whom every family in heaven and on earth is named . . .

It is important that we look at ourselves, discover or test our motives, and I expect we do fall into many traps. But it certainly could not be said to be true that God the Father acted in a 'paternalistic' way towards his Son Jesus. Many would also conclude that he could not be a good Father to have allowed his Son into this situation. Here is a deep mystery, which calls for much prayer, meditation and personal involvement with God, Father, Son and Holy Spirit. That is why St Paul continues:

. . . that according to the riches of his glory he may grant you to be strengthened with might through his Spirit in the inner man, and that Christ may dwell in your hearts through faith; that you, being rooted and grounded in love, may have power to comprehend with all the saints what is the breadth and length and height and depth, and to know the love of Christ which surpasses knowledge, that you may be filled with all the fullness of God.

(Ephesians 3:14–19)

Perhaps too at this point when we think of all Jesus has to fill us with, and we read: 'for our sake he made him to be sin', we can more fully realize what it means when we read that he emptied himself (Philippians 2:5–7).

Given our own sin, our own falls, are we humble enough to follow the stumbling Jesus along the way?

Meditation   Psalm 127 [126]:1–2.

Jesus falls a second time

VII

(ii)

'Take heart, my son; your sins are forgiven. And behold, some of the scribes said to themselves, 'This man is blaspheming.' But Jesus, knowing their thoughts, said, 'Why do you think evil in your hearts? For which is easier, to say, "Your sins are forgiven," or to say, "Rise and walk"? But that you may know that the Son of man has authority on earth to forgive sins' — he then said to the paralytic — 'Rise, take up your bed and go home.' And he rose and went home.

(Matthew 9:2–7)

I expect that as long as the world has existed, and men and women have lived upon its surface, there have been the wide ranges of sickness which exist today. They are not necessarily all apparent at a particular age, and some marvellous discoveries have been made over the years. But such basic things as nervousness, guilt, pride, self-depreciation, depression and a tendency to suicide are always about somewhere beneath the surface.

Christ in his mission to us brought with him a great power of healing. It is ironic that when he hangs on the Cross they more or less cry out to him: 'Physician, heal yourself', which he had quoted in the synagogue after he had read from the book about his mission under the Spirit to preach the good news to the poor. There he had added, 'Truly, I say to you, no prophet is acceptable in his own country' (Luke 4:16–30).

But the major exercise of his healing resulted from the inner faith of the one to be healed, and was combined with the forgiveness of sin. In other words, the physical fall or disunity or disease was closely associated with spiritual fall or sickness.

As we witness the sinless one made sin for us, and falling under the weight of the Cross, there is a good opportunity for us to step back, and to take a look into ourselves as whole people . . . or should I say people who should be whole, and are not!

Each one of us is in need of healing in some way or another. In humility we must recognize that fact of life, and then set about our approach to Jesus, to his love, to his healing and to our own personal reconciliation. The moment of fall can be the moment of truth. Jesus is telling us on this way of his to Calvary that the way we must follow will be one where inevitably we will fall. But he wants us on our part to make it inevitable —

by prayer, fasting and almsgiving, done in a spirit of faith and love — that we also have the courage to get up and go on. He is there ahead of us. He is here with us.

Prayer   Psalm 134 [133].

WEDNESDAY

The Daughters of Jerusalem weep for Jesus (i)

And there followed him a great multitude of the people, and of women who bewailed and lamented him.

(Luke 23:27)

Only one evangelist mentions this incident on the way of the Cross — St Luke. His own origins and the origins of his writings are of course disputed territory, but he does hit at his sources:

Inasmuch as many have undertaken to compile a narrative of the things which have been accomplished among us, just as they were delivered to us by those who from the beginning were eyewitnesses and ministers of the word . . .

(Luke 1:1–2)

Luke is seen as the companion of Paul on some of his journeys, and to Rome. He is supposed to have been a Gentile converted to Christianity.

But Paul himself was not known as being at the crucifixion, and Luke has his own version of the narrative of the Passion. Another theory is that he was close to the Virgin Mary, from whom he derived the basis for the birth/infancy stories and also perhaps for the different slant on the Passion.

One interesting vision is contained in the report that a great multitude followed along the way, but to the women is given the outward expression of their dismay, sorrow and pity. We all know how easy it is to collect a crowd even for a murder trial or something sordid in sexual offence. In the past people have gathered for public executions, as they still do in parts of Asia. We cannot therefore say that those who followed in crowds were on

Jesus' side. They may equally have been wanting to see the two thieves executed with Jesus, because they were after blood, not justice.

This brings up the purpose of Luke's writing, which is to make clear over and over again that Jesus' purpose in living, dying and rising is to teach the universal love and forgiveness of God. What God wants from us is our readiness to listen and a willingness to act (Isaiah 1:16–18).

The women were in reality out there to meet Jesus in defence of the fatherless, seeking justice, correcting oppression as best they could. After all, had not Jesus said, as it were on their behalf:

'The scribes and the Pharisees sit on Moses' seat; so practise and observe whatever they tell you, but not what they do; for they preach, but do not practise. They bind heavy burdens, hard to bear, and lay them on men's shoulders; but they themselves will not move them with their finger.'

(Matthew 23:2–4)

Today as ever, there are many voiceless people — voiceless not because they cannot speak, but because they cannot be heard. This applies inside the Church as well as in society. When Jesus was about in the land, he spoke for his people; he had a voice that the establishment listened to. They did not like what they heard, and this was why he was now carrying his cross. He had dared to criticize, to speak out of line with the common pattern and policy. He had given hope to the poor, spoken against injustice, tried to lift oppression. And he left us an example and a message: Follow me! But Jesus wept for Jerusalem (Matthew 23:37–39). In losing Jesus to the power of the chief priests, the women of Jerusalem indeed had something to weep over.

What should we be weeping about in our life and society?

Meditation   Isaiah 1:16–18.

✠ The Daughters of Jerusalem
Ⅷ weep for Jesus (ii)

But Jesus turning to them said, 'Daughters of Jerusalem, do not weep for me, but weep for yourselves and for your children. For behold, the days are coming when they will say, "Blessed are the barren, and the wombs that never bore, and the breasts that never gave suck!"'

(Luke 23:28–29)

Jesus Christ was all the time given to his Father's will and to other people. Our own human and deep-rooted focal point is self. The Spanish soldier of the sixteenth century who found God through reading the Bible when he was laid low by a battle wound and had nothing else to read — Ignatius Loyola — used to say that the greatest battle in life is against self. And self dies half an hour after we do!

Jesus then is a great lesson to us all along the way. Here, when he is himself battered and *in extremis*, the evangelist tells us that he still has thought for those who are lamenting him and pitying him in his awful condition.

'Weep for yourselves and for your children.' Though he was himself about to go through a tortured death which would bring liberation in the resurrection, he knew full well that the trials and wars, poverties and oppressions of human existence would go on. As we look about us we are bound to admit that he was right.

If we were Old Testament people, we could possibly have lived at the time of one of the prophets. At random, we could have heard someone like Ezekiel holding forth in the name of the Lord:

'Because the land is full of bloody crimes and the city is full of violence, I will bring the worst of the nations to take possession of their houses . . . and they shall know that I am the LORD.'

(Ezekiel 7:23–24, 27; cp. Jeremiah 6:22–23)

This is not to get ourselves into total gloom during the period of Lent, but it is to remind us that things such as this were said in the past, before Jesus. Jesus himself said much, including the difficulty of making any impression. (See his parable of Dives and Lazarus, which ends: 'if they do not hear Moses and the prophets, neither will they be convinced if someone should rise from the dead' — Luke 16:19–31.) And down the ages similar appeals and warnings have been given. Indeed, there are voices in many places today which are stressing the appalling nature of hunger in the world, where millions die each year of malnutrition or starvation, while other millions barely subsist. At the same time many millions and billions of pounds are spent on armaments and actual warfare.

Some of the Churches and their members are very insistent that theirs is only a spiritual role. There should be no interference in the worldly matters which border on politics and are not the concern of the Church. Nevertheless, there are those, myself among them, who believe strongly that Jesus' option for the poor was a very real intervention, from which we must not withdraw; that he was most concerned with justice, and he left this message behind him, to be echoed by James (5:1–6) and by many of his followers from that time to this.

What is our option for the poor as we follow Jesus and recall that one of the features of Lent is almsgiving, which in this sense covers a much wider aspect — not merely giving the widow's mite, but questioning fundamental attitudes in government and ourselves?

Prayer   Psalm 86 [85]:1–4.

FRIDAY

The Daughters of Jerusalem weep for Jesus (iii)

'Then they will begin to say to the mountains, "Fall on us"; and to the hills, "Cover us".'

(Luke 23:30; cp. Mark 11:22–25)

It is possible for us to get into moods, to feel depression, to lose heart, even to give up altogether and turn in upon ourselves, and away from God. I have known that personally, and still do, especially when I am faced with the apparently insurmountable problems which turn up in people's lives. Unfortunately, it is not easy to illustrate very directly what I mean, without breaking confidences, and to make general complaints about injustice and so on really does not help anyone.

In giving the word of Jesus to the women of Jerusalem, I want it to be clear that there are more sides than one to his message. The love of God which is universal and everlasting is both a strong and a gentle love. In gentleness he can speak:

> **My beloved speaks and says to me:**
> **'Arise, my love, my fair one, and come away;**
> **for lo, the winter is past,**
> **the rain is over and gone.**
> **The flowers appear on the earth,**
> **the time for singing has come,**
> **and the voice of the turtledove**
> **is heard in our land.'**
>
> (Song of Solomon 2:10–12)

But the Lord is not just a 'sugar daddy', about with us to pet and spoil us. He treats us as he has made us — as human beings with minds, hearts and wills of our own. It is up to us to listen, or not — to pray or not, to act on his commands or not (Mark 11:22–25).

Our responsibility remains what it has always been since the revelation to Adam and Eve — the responsibility for the earth (Genesis 3:23). Unfortunately, even in the first days with Cain and Abel (Genesis 4:2–8), relationships between human beings began to go sour and in the subsequent development, the love of God in its strength was often seen as the anger of God, so that frequently God appears as a very changeable person. The reality is that we change, while all history is the song of God's love — a love which needs to train and discipline and asks at the same time for mankind's faith and love.

In Moses we find his faith tested, but he resorts to prayer, and his prayer wins through (e.g. Deuteronomy 9–10). The same is true of the famous prayer of Abraham for Sodom (Genesis 18:22–33). We should look at the women of Jerusalem and their grief, measure it and our own times when God has seemed to abandon us, and then turn to the messages of hope and faith which come through Scripture.

There are many people about and many occasions we come across in daily life where the greatest thing which we can do, for ourselves and the others, is to live in complete faith and trust. I don't doubt that for a great number of people, the mountain does not seem to be removed, but stays obstinately in place. However, strangely, faith grows stronger if it is tested, and we must be humble under that test, and go on hoping. In this we can help one another, even when our own faith seems weak.

Prayer Questioner: Dear God, prayer is grey, dull, empty and almost boring. I cannot believe that I am praying at all, though I know I want to pray.

God: You must accept the prayer that I give you. You are praying as a member of my body and you are sharing in the dull emptiness which so many experience today. With me you bear the burdens of others as others help to bear yours. Have courage and keep on, for I am with you always even in the greyest prayer.

SATURDAY

The Daughters of Jerusalem weep for Jesus (iv)

'For if they do this when the wood is green, what will happen when it is dry?'

(Luke 23:31)

The interpretation of the quotation from Luke is taken as being a reference to the innocence of Jesus as the green over against the guilty depicted as dry. It might also be taken in regard to the development down the ages or the failure to develop. Jesus knows what it is to be condemned as an innocent person. In his own life he has spent much of his time in forgiving sins and doing what he could for those unjustly accused.

Meeting these women must have been a joy, because they were genuinely grieving for him and not accusing him.

One of the famous unjust accusations is told in the story of Susanna, but on that occasion Daniel raised his voice in protest, and turned the false accusation back on the accusers (Daniel 13 or Susanna 44–64). No one appeared in this way for Jesus.

We can see in his behaviour with the scribes and Pharisees and the woman taken in adultery how kind but firm he could be. He refused to condemn her, he refused to throw a stone at her, and he sent her away, with the admonition to sin no more (John 8:4–11).

Our law has always been supposed to uphold that a man is innocent until he is proved guilty. But we are now in the middle of a very rough sea as far as justice is concerned.

The advent of mass media has made things more difficult, because there can almost be trial by TV, or in the newspaper. There are areas where there is much injustice, particularly in arrests and cases concerning oppressed minority groups, as widely diverse as the black people and the homosexual. But there are others as well who get pursued by journalists, are talked about all over the place and really suffer immensely from whispering. Sadly, among the worst offenders in this are regular churchgoers.

It is remarkable how much good, on the other hand, can come from a positive and friendly approach, especially to a person who is out of tune with himself or his thinking. It has been one of the anxieties turned to joy and growth in my life to have had the privilege to be a considerable amount in the company of people from the West Indies and India. I have found this a very rich experience spiritually, culturally and in friendship. I can say with equal sincerity that I have gained a great deal from my work with those who are mentally or physically handicapped, more especially the mentally handicapped. They so often have insights of a simplicity and depth which take my breath away. But in addition to this, I would add that my many contacts with individual homosexuals, male and female, have opened my mind to understand, to share the tension some endure, the joy and fulfilment some find and the sense of anger when they are persecuted. Finally, from alcoholics, drug addicts and thieves I have also gained. I can understand Jesus moving in strange company to the scandal of others!

Meditation   Colossians 1:15–23.

The New Covenant and the Grain of Wheat

'This is the covenant which I will make with the house of Israel after those days, says the LORD: I will put my law within them, and I will write it upon their hearts; and I will be their God, and they shall be my people. And no longer shall each man teach his neighbour and each his brother, saying, "Know the LORD," for they shall all know me, from the least of them to the greatest, says the LORD; for I will forgive their iniquity, and I will remember their sin no more.'

(Jeremiah 31:33–34)

'Truly, truly, I say unto you, unless a grain of wheat falls into the earth and dies, it remains alone; but if it dies, it bears much fruit.'

(John 12:24)

The theme of the covenant points now directly to the new covenant of Jesus Christ, which we shall share in our Holy Week and Easter liturgy.

The prophecy of the covenant from Jeremiah and the words of Jesus Christ help us to ponder the cost of discipleship, for ourselves personally in the light of the total cost to Christ. Are we taking the lesson of Lent seriously? Is this period of re-assessment and repentance really going to make any impression on our way of life?

In this last week before Holy Week, without making a lot of resolutions which we may not keep, it would be a good idea to review what we have learnt and what has penetrated our being since we responded to the call of Ash Wednesday. Is it our hearts, not our garments, which have been torn open?

Jesus is not only our teacher, our brother and our God. For those who were with him during his life, he was the sacrament, the daily revelation of the active power of God's love in the life of the world. He remains the sacrament for us in the Church. Each of us should confess our sins, even those who do not accept confession as a sacrament. We must examine ourselves deeply to join in the spirit of repentance in the gospel and the purpose of the Lenten season. Some have a priest or counsellor who can help them, others have a particular friend of whom one says, 'He/she knows me through and through'. Surely the Lord knows me through and through? Yes, indeed, but also, each of us can cloud our recognition of God's still small voice, if we are alone in listening to his judgement: 'He who states his case first seems right until the other comes and examines him . . . A brother helped is like a strong city' (Proverbs 18:17,19).

In these days of intensifying communication through press and other media, we are not necessarily communicating with each other better, or even as well, as we did before. Sometimes, prayer groups are a useful medium, helping us to open up and express our needs, fears and insights. Group discussions are also a growing blessing, if you can discover your way into one. But often, the deepest and best is the personal, one-to-one and regular exchanges with a trusted 'soul friend'. In opening up to another, we are in a way dying to ourselves, but a great harvest can come through this death.

Meditation   Philippians 2:1–11.

MONDAY

Jesus falls a third time

Then Peter came up and said to him, 'Lord, how often shall my brother sin against me, and I forgive him? As many as seven times?' Jesus said to him, 'I do not say to you seven times, but seventy times seven.'

(Matthew 18:21–22)

When, in meditating on the way of the Cross, I come to the third and last fall of Jesus, my mind and heart open to Christ in deep gratitude. I'll tell you why! I am myself a recurrent sinner!

We know that the law is spiritual; but I am carnal, sold under sin. I do not understand my own actions. For I do not do what I want, but I do the very thing I hate. Now if I do what I do not want, I agree that the law is good.

(Romans 7:14–16)

I am no St Paul; I'm just a sinner. However, looking at the fall of Christ and his getting up and going on, I can go on with St Paul:

Wretched man that I am! Who will deliver me from this body of

death? Thanks be to God through Jesus Christ our Lord! So then, I of myself serve the law of God with my mind, but with my flesh I serve the law of sin.

(Romans 7:24–25)

The third fall of Jesus shows the weakness of the flesh, not in a sinful way, but as part of the human weakness. There is great hope for most of us who have a regular and personal failing which we have to confess to God all too regularly.

We can become discouraged. We say to ourselves: 'What is the use of going on? I'll only do it again (or fail again to do what I should); I'm beyond redemption.' And then we pack it in and just drift along without God.

When Peter asks Jesus about forgiving, Jesus' reply is God's reply. It is the reply of everlasting and merciful love, for he — the Lord God — has made us out of love, and he knows our weakness . . . and he still loves us.

It is told of G. K. Chesterton, who was a very large and stout person, that he once arrived to debate upon the theme that things are not always what they seem to be. He stood there to speak, looking grossly overweight — spoke the theme of the debate, then proceeded to stop and take a couple of pillows out from under his pullover!

Others can see us very differently from the way we know ourselves to be. But Jesus knows us. Jesus goes on loving us as we slip and fall and get up and go on. I believe all he says to us is, 'Go on trying! When you fall turn to me in sorrow and love, and get up and try again. You will fall again, I have no doubt! All right! Try again! I am always with you until the end of time.'

Now I want you to try to spread this good news to others who may have lost hope, gone out on the fringe of things, feel swamped with vice, alcoholism, violence, sex, disbelief. For each and every one there is still the patience of God shown in Jesus' falling and slow painful rising to his feet again as he staggers up along the way of the Cross.

A great deal more needs to be done for the despairing of this world. The ones who have turned off, given up, called it a day, denied the existence of the goodness of God. As we face this third fall of Jesus Christ, especially if we are sad, disillusioned ourselves, let us have the courage, the patience and the love to drag ourselves up again to follow Jesus, giving a helping hand to anyone who needs it.

Prayer Psalm 62 [61]:5–8.

Jesus is stripped of his garments (i)

They divided his garments among them by casting lots.

(Matthew 27:35)

'Learn from me; for I am gentle and lowly in heart.'

(Matthew 11:29)

The evangelists do not mention this part of the crucifixion as such. The reference comes later, when Christ has actually been crucified and the soldiers get on with sharing out the spoils as part of their 'perks' for the job which they have done. We therefore simply assume that he was stripped, since his garments were there for division.

There is something fundamentally humiliating in persons being stripped of clothing, if they have learnt to wear clothing. There are comparatively few who go totally naked in the world. I am ignorant, but I remember the Karamojo when I was in Uganda and there may be other tribes elsewhere. The degree of covering varies. What is decent for one area or generation may be indecent for another. But unless the usual pattern of behaviour is complete nakedness, there is a social or cultural significance in wearing something nowadays in most places.

We read of Noah's drunkenness which led to his sons seeing his nakedness as he lay unclothed. Ham got cursed because he told his brothers. They discreetly covered their father. Leviticus has quite a lot to say about nakedness, mostly in regard to forms of illicit intercourse (Leviticus 20:17–21).

What I am trying to say is that there is nothing awful or sinful about the human body or nakedness, but stripping publicly against the will of the person stripped is a gross indignity.

This is the indignity which Jesus suffered before he was crucified. In a way, it was no worse than scourging, crowning, being condemned to death, being given his cross to carry. It is as though he had got on to a computered programme which read 'crucifixion' — and after that the system just went into gear. But the humiliation is no less — the degradation of having clothes stripped from you by soldiers who perhaps think of you as an animal to be baited and played with.

That is what Jesus went through for us. The only way is to ask you to imagine yourself unjustly accused and then taken out to Tower Hill, Notting Hill, Kensington High Street, Manchester Piccadilly, Liverpool

Lime Street, Cardiff Castle, Edinburgh, anywhere . . . and there being stripped.

Jesus went through it. Whatever translation you have about the phrase he uses of himself — humble, meek, lowly . . . it all comes to the same thing — he did not protest. He went through with it with all that it meant.

Where does that leave us? Jesus echoes Lamentations 3:25, 27, 30 . . . 'If any one strikes you on the right cheek, turn to him the other also' (Matthew 5:39).

I think we all hope that we will not be submitted to such indignity. If we were, some of us would come through with dignity, others would just crack up. No matter! If we have got this far, so that we are at the point of crucifixion on Calvary, we have had that amount of courage, of faithfulness and of compassion to come this far. Let us be quite sure that the Lord will help us to go further, so that through his message of peace, unity and love will gradually prevail, no matter what the ups and downs.

Prayer Psalm 55[54]:1–8.

WEDNESDAY

Jesus is stripped of his garments (ii)

And they crucified him, and divided his garments among them, casting lots for them, to decide what each should take.

(Mark 15:24)

'Take Aaron and Eleazar . . . and bring them up to Mount Hor; and strip Aaron of his garments and put them upon Eleazar his son; and Aaron shall be gathered to his people, and shall die there.' Moses did as the LORD commanded; and they went up Mount Hor in the sight of all the congregation. And Moses stripped Aaron of his garments, and put them upon Eleazar . . . And Aaron died there on the top of the mountain.

(Numbers 20:25–28)

The stripping of Jesus when he came to Calvary was very different from that commanded by God for Aaron. Of course, Aaron had been in trouble as Moses had been at the waters of Meribah (Numbers 20:2–13) and so was to die before entering the promised land. His stripping too was in preparation for his death, but his clothes were handed on for a purpose, the continuance of his priestly office.

As we see Jesus stripped, let us refer this to our own selves, not so much in a physical way, but in a material and spiritual way. Job laments:

'He has walled up my way, so that I cannot pass,
and he has set darkness upon my paths.
He has stripped from me my glory,
and taken the crown from my head.'

(Job 19:8–9)

But before that when his trials had first come upon him, he laid down the fundamental principles of dependence upon God in our lives.

Then Job arose, and rent his robe, and shaved his head, and fell upon the ground, and worshipped. And he said, 'Naked I came from my mother's womb, and naked shall I return; the LORD gave, and the LORD has taken away; blessed be the name of the LORD.'

(Job 1:20–21)

We collect material things round us. Part of the essence of religious life has been to follow a vow of poverty after the example of Jesus. The disciples felt the rub of following Christ themselves and at one stage began to seek for some security, after Jesus had spoken out to the rich young man and told him to sell everything and follow him (Luke 18:18–30).

It is valuable to look around oneself and try to get a perspective in relation to God in Jesus' word, and in relation to others in the world. I find it salutary to turn out what I possess, giving away all that seems possible — or rather more! It is a kind of spiritual spring-cleaning.

At such times, as I see Jesus stripped and see my own nature of hoarding and acquiring, I think of St Francis of Assisi. You remember he stripped himself in front of his father of his ordinary but rich clothing, and started his call from Christ, naked. Later, when those Francis had called to the poverty of Christ could not take it, they relieved him of the governance of the followers. Francis, however, remained true to his call and insisted on being placed naked on the ground to die.

Lent is the part of Jesus' stripping process in our lives which we should take seriously. It can change our thinking and our life-style. It may be permanent or only temporary. But if there is no deep impact this year, by God's grace, there will always be next year!

Prayer   Psalm 84 [83]:10–12.

Jesus is nailed to the Cross

XI

There they crucified him, and with the two others, one on either side, and Jesus between them. Pilate also wrote a title and put it on the cross; it read, 'Jesus of Nazareth, the King of the Jews.' Many of the Jews read this title, for the place where Jesus was crucified was near the city; and it was written in Hebrew, in Latin and in Greek. The chief priests of the Jews then said to Pilate, 'Do not write, "The King of the Jews" but, "This man said, I am the King of the Jews."' Pilate answered, 'What I have written I have written' . . .

But standing by the cross of Jesus were his mother, and his mother's sister, Mary the wife of Clopas, and Mary Magdalene. When Jesus saw his mother, and the disciple whom he loved standing near, he said to his mother, 'Woman, behold, your son!' Then he said to his disciple, 'Behold, your mother!' And from that hour the disciple took her to his own home.

(John 19:18–22, 25–27)

I am anticipating the crucifixion and death of Jesus by one week for the purpose of our meditation on the way of the Cross because with Holy Week we enter an intense, close-packed ordeal of living out the last days of Jesus' life all over again. I think by our preview of what is to happen, we can establish certain thoughts in our minds and allow them to settle there while we go over the way of the Cross again next week.

What has your experience been of the crucifixion? Is it real to you, or very distant? For me, for a time, it was very distant, even absent, but Jesus met me again on the Way of the Cross in Jerusalem, so that I then sat for hour upon hour amid the surging crowds in the Church of the Holy Sepulchre — and I can only say the cross was real. In recent years we have re-enacted the Way of the Cross through the streets and estates of Notting Hill.

Those who enter the drama in Notting Hill are themselves sharing Christ's suffering in their own lives, and helping to give the message to anyone who is standing by. We are all of us witnesses to the crucifixion and the resurrection, because we have been marked with the sign of the cross. Think for a minute about the group at the cross. Who got there? Mary, mother of Jesus, whom we think had already met him on the way.

She loved him through everything, and his tender loving care for her is shown when he puts her in the charge of John. John too is there. John is also carried there by love, for love is strong to overcome fear. And there is Mary Magdalene. She too is drawn by the love Jesus had poured out to her, and she has love springing up inside her like living waters. We learn the lesson of love at the foot of the cross, held there not by fear or a sense of guilt, but simply love. Jesus, brother and Lord, saviour and lover, has the greatest love of all . . . to give his life for his Father's will to be fulfilled — so that we, the unlovable, may each of us be filled with that pardon and peace, kindling fires of love in us.

Meditation John 15:9–14.

FRIODAY

Jesus dies on the Cross

After this Jesus, knowing that all was now finished, said (to fulfil the scripture), 'I thirst.' A bowl of vinegar stood there; so they put a sponge full of the vinegar on hyssop and held it to his mouth. When Jesus had received the vinegar, he said, 'It is finished'; and he bowed his head and gave up his spirit.

(John 19:28–30)

It is deeply painful to sit by the bedside of someone who is dying from a painful cancer or some other disease from which the agony cannot be entirely removed. Yet, I have found it not unusual to be torn in two directions. On the one hand, I rebel against the moment of death and want to postpone it as long as possible, for a last word, a last embrace, a last smile, the very sense that he or she is still there. On the other hand, I cannot wait for the pain to end, for a new peace to spread over the beloved face, for a move into my faith that there is eternal life beyond death. What must have been the feelings at the foot of the cross? It cannot be counted out that those present still thought there might be a miracle. We do not know. The chief priests and passers-by, Mark tells us, mocked (Mark 15:29–32).

For his followers it was a terrible blow. In Jesus' death, their source of hope had gone. What was left? I don't think we can tell. It is not worthwhile to speculate. Just think how such a blow would hit you!

We, who live as Easter people in the faith of the risen Christ have not the same emptiness, though I admit I often find the morning of Holy Saturday very 'empty' somehow.

Let us concentrate on the death of Jesus in one or two ways. Firstly, after all the struggle and the pain, Jesus has brought his human nature to the point of the final fulfilment of his Father's will: 'It is finished'. The way of the Cross, which began from his birth and was accentuated at his decision-making in the forty nights and days in the desert, is now completed.

'Brother will deliver up brother to death, and the father his child, and children will rise against parents and have them put to death; and you will be hated by all for my name's sake. But he who endures to the end will be saved.'

(Matthew 10:21–22)

These sober words of warning by Jesus we can easily put to one side, but witnessing to his death as we meditate before the scene of the crucifixion reminds us of the reality of what happened to him, and how he did indeed endure to the end. There are no short cuts to eternal life. Each of us must persevere. We can help one another. Jesus and his Spirit will help us. But we must go on. And lest we should get in despair and feel it is all too much to be asked of us, we have Jesus' words of comfort:

'Fear not, little flock, for it is your Father's good pleasure to give you the kingdom.'

(Luke 12:32)

And let us also as we look on Jesus hanging and dying on the cross recall again the wonderful words of St Paul:

He destined us in love to be his sons through Jesus Christ, according to the purpose of his will, to the praise of his glorious grace which he freely bestowed on us in the Beloved. In him we have redemption through his blood, the forgiveness of our trespasses, according to the riches of his grace which he lavished upon us.'

(Ephesians 1:5–8)

At Jesus' baptism, God spoke:

'This is my beloved Son, with whom I am well pleased.'

(Matthew 3:17)

At the moment of Transfiguration, God said:

'This is my son, my Chosen; listen to him!'

(Luke 9:35)

At Calvary, there was no intelligible word, only darkness and the splitting of the veil of the temple . . . but surely God was saying in the silence of eternity: 'This is my Son, my Beloved, with whom I am well pleased.'

Prayer   Psalm 150.

SATURDAY

✝ Preparing for Jerusalem, and the Way of the Cross

From that time Jesus began to show his disciples that he must go to Jerusalem and suffer many things from the elders and chief priests and scribes, and be killed, and on the third day raised. And Peter took him and began to rebuke him, saying, 'God forbid, Lord! This shall never happen to you.' But he turned and said to Peter, 'Get behind me, Satan! You are a hindrance to me; for you are not on the side of God, but of men.'

(Matthew 16:21–23; cp. Luke 9:51–56)

We prepare for Christ's entry into Jerusalem as celebrated on Palm Sunday. The disciples had begun the preparation some time before. Jesus had not hidden from them the general outline of what was to happen to him in Jerusalem, but it does not seem from the accounts by the evangelists that they really grasped the full import of what he was saying . . . at least, Peter may have done, but thought for a time he could persuade Jesus into a different direction. Judas may also have had his plan for redirecting Jesus' way to power.

The disciples were very close to Jesus, witnessing his preaching and miracles. They may have been cushioned against the hostility which he aroused. James and John were indignant when the Samaritan village would not allow Christ in, and suggested to him that they should get fire to come down from heaven. This brought a rebuke from Christ, but I ask myself if they learnt from the incident anything of the opposition and hatred which was growing.

We can be blind, can't we? I believe Rome was blind at the time of the Reformation, and deaf as well. When I was in Nicaragua in 1984, one of the priests was telling me how he had warned the Archbishop before the revolution that it was imminent, and had been told to get on with his work, as it was nonsense to talk that way. It may be that there are issues today over which there is blindness or deafness — the position of women, including ordination, or in the Roman Catholic Church permission for the use of general absolution — these among other things. Perhaps, above all, we are being blind to nuclear escalation, present and future ecological problems . . . and perhaps on our very own doorsteps the desperate plight of people is being overlooked, with clear pleas falling on deaf ears.

A whole area in which we can be blind and deaf as Christians is that of Christian living. Just as the disciples did not want to face hostility and did not want Jesus to live dangerously, so the Churches, of which I and you are part, are not willing to court unpopularity with their diminishing number of followers by preaching what some might consider radical.

Jesus went to Jerusalem, against his follower's judgement. Jesus prepared to enter in triumph, knowing that this triumph had to be put behind him as another trap of Satan.

Meditation   Luke 19:41–46.

PALM OR PASSION SUNDAY

✝ Jesus rejects worldly power

The disciples went and did as Jesus had directed them; they brought the ass and the colt, and put their garments on them, and he sat thereon. Most of the crowd spread their garments on the road, and others cut branches from the trees and spread them on the road. And the crowds that went before him and that followed him shouted, 'Hosanna to the Son of David! Blessed is he who comes in the name of the Lord! Hosanna in the highest!' And when he entered Jerusalem, all the city was stirred, saying, 'Who is this?' And the crowds said, 'This is the prophet Jesus from Nazareth of Galilee.'

(Matthew 21:6–11)

Palm Sunday opens the Holy Week which leads to Easter Sunday through the full drama of the Passion and death of Jesus Christ. We take ourselves back in our meditation on the way of the Cross to enter into the preliminaries once more. This helps us to remember the meaning of the long approach to Jerusalem and Jesus' death, which spans the whole of the Old Testament and Christ's life. Please read Zechariah 9:9–10.

For any who picked up the implications of what was happening, this would have been a great boost of hope that the Roman domination would now be overthrown, that this prophet from Nazareth was indeed the one they had been waiting for.

The power movements in Israel had waxed and waned. There had been the early entering of the promised land, with the similar miracle of the holding back of the waters as at the Exodus (Exodus 14 and Joshua 3), through to the might of Saul, David and Solomon, told in 2 Samuel and 1 Kings. Always there was the combined hope of the restoration of earthly power and the Messiah who had God with him.

Jesus had already rejected this 'worldly' approach, when he struggled with Satan in the desert (Matthew 4:1–11).

But the disciples had never quite come to understand that, and even when Jesus had risen they were still looking for an earthly kingdom (Acts 1:6).

Now Jesus accepted the shouts of the crowd, which he had already heard in his ears both for him and against him. He had to avoid that crowd which wished to destroy him at Nazareth (Luke 4:28–30), but so many had also thronged to him and acclaimed his miracles.

Not only the disciples but we ourselves can get confused by the methods and designs of God. Again and again we like to seek our approbation and to make a success of something. Indeed, it seems pretty hopeless simply to expect failure. On the other hand our closeness to Jesus and his ability to open our eyes will help that detachment which is essential if we are to find the will of God through the tangle of human affairs and human emotions.

Prayer   Psalm 86 [85]:8–13.

MONDAY OF HOLY WEEK

✝ Between Palm Sunday and the Way of the Cross (i)

Every day he was teaching in the temple, but at night he went out and lodged on the mount callet Olivet. And early in the morning all the people came to him in the temple to hear him.

(Luke 21:37–38)

Jesus filled the days between his triumphal entry into Jerusalem and eating the Passover with his disciples by teaching in the temple. At night he went off to the Mount of Olives. What exactly it means when the text says 'lodged' there is not clear to me. From my own experience when I was a soldier in Palestine, it was perfectly possible to 'lodge' anywhere during the warmer months. Lodging for us at that time simply meant finding a nice quiet place, putting a haversack on the ground, and then lying down under the stars and sleeping exceedingly well!

This must have been a very frustrating time for the scribes and Pharisees, because Jesus was in the temple each day. When he came in, the crowds gathered round him and listened to what he had to say, more intently than to their own teachers. The scribes and Pharisees tried to wrest the authority of teaching back from him by questioning him and seeking discussion as it were on their own ground.

This misfired! He was asked, By what authority? He answered with a question (Luke 20:2–8). When they could not answer it, he refused to talk about his authority.

He made a very clear reference to himself in the parable of the man who planted a vineyard (Luke 20:9–18) — but the scribes and Pharisees recognized that it was also pointed at them! So he continued to annoy them by his straight talk.

How do we behave when we are up against some point of disagreement or discussion? Do we try to wriggle out by understatements? Do we bluster our way through? Do we speak calmly and objectively, trying to win by truth?

One of the wonderful things about Jesus is that we do not have to follow his pattern action for action. We are free to make our choice. If we are prayerful, we will pray what we decide and what we do will be in line with God's will. But *we* make the decision, and hence the need to be well steeped in prayer so that we can know, underneath somewhere, the secret of God's plan.

Meditation   Psalm 1:1–3.

TUESDAY OF HOLY WEEK

Between Palm Sunday and the Way of the Cross (ii)

One of the scribes came up and heard them disputing with one another, and seeing that he answered them well, asked him, 'Which commandment is the first of all?' Jesus answered, 'The first is, "Hear, O Israel: The Lord our God, the Lord is one; and you shall love the Lord your God with all your heart, and with all your soul, and with all your mind, and with all your strength." The second is this, "You shall love your neighbour as yourself." There is no other commandment greater than these.'

(Mark 12:28–31)

Jesus used the short period between Palm Sunday and the way of the Cross, for some very important teaching.

Today's reading is one of those teachings. We know it so well, we can almost push it off to one side. But it is so important, each of us should take time off this Holy Week to sit in front of God and this commandment — to just let God and his will sink into our very being. This is meditation, this is contemplation. Let yourself be deeply submerged in the commandment, so that it touches your inner parts, and gives you power to love where it is difficult to love.

Jesus was in some way aware that the time was drawing near. He also knew that there was discontent in Judas, even treachery and possible betrayal; yet he kept on with his ordinary round, giving himself in word and example.

Have you ever been in a situation where you are waiting for an inevitable development, a D-Day, when something less than pleasant hanging over you will become a reality? It can be terrible! There is a gloom over everything, because the gloom is deep inside. Occasionally, it is possible to forget in other busy-ness, in interesting events. But then — a moment of lull, of nothing immediate to do, and the gloom envelops everything again like a fog. Or, when you get to sleep and wake at three or four in the morning it is there again, causing a dread and a frustration to all hope of further sleep.

Jesus just went on doing his Father's will. Later he was to sweat it out in the Garden of Gethsemane, reminding us that this was not a sudden realization of what was to come, but the eruption of that darkness which had been with him all the time while he was in and out of Jerusalem, giving comfort to others, praising the generosity of the widow and her mite, using what time he had left.

This is the epitome of what St Paul means when he says: 'Love is patient' (1 Corinthians 13:4). We come into situations ourselves when we are quite out of step with others, but we must keep going on. We may have occasion in married living or in our work when there is a general blight over everything we do or touch — no peace, no joy, no satisfaction, no sense of loving or being loved. Our temptation? To pack it all up! What we must do . . . follow Jesus to Jerusalem, to the Garden of Gethsemane, to the way of the Cross . . . follow, follow, follow!

Meditation   Psalm 91 [90]:1–6.

The Last Supper

And when the hour came, he sat at table, and the apostles with him. And he said to them, 'I have earnestly desired to eat this Passover with you before I suffer.'
(Luke 22:14–15)

Jesus . . . rose from supper, laid aside his garments, and girded himself with a towel. Then he poured water into a basin, and began to wash the disciples' feet, and to wipe them with the towel with which he was girded.
(John 13:3–5)

And as they were eating, he took bread, and blessed, and broke it, and gave it to them, and said, 'Take; this is my body.' And he took a cup, and when he had given thanks he gave it to them, and they all drank of it. And he said to them, 'This is my blood of the covenant, which is poured out for many.'
(Mark 14:22–24)

We celebrate this beautiful story tomorrow, but then I want to think about the other part of Maundy Thursday — Gethsemane. So today we look at the two parts of the meal, both acts of service by Jesus to his friends.

I am always deeply moved by the words Luke attributed to Jesus, 'I have earnestly desired to eat this Passover with you before I suffer.' We have all of us, I imagine, had a poignant parting in life. In my experience, such times vary in their content and their pain. Sometimes I find myself so full up, there is little or nothing to say — just a dumb silence, or hugging or crying. At other times there is just so much I want to say, to clear up, to share before parting.

We know from John (13–17) that Jesus was in the second category, because we have a rich legacy from him to his friends before he leaves them. These chapters in themselves could be meditation enough for Lent or a lifetime!

The words always make me aware of the difficulties of parting, especially when death is involved. To keep silent and hide dying from a person seems kind and may be. But there is also the other side, and I would ask you to give some thought to it in regard to yourself and those near you. I have found such joy and peace from the sharing of the terminal nature of a person's illness and passage to death. Subsequently, it is also a great aid to the person left behind, the bereaved. There *are* pros and cons. Pray over them yourself.

Of Jesus' service in washing the feet of his friends let me only say that this is the hallmark of the incarnation and one which is to be at the forefront of our Christian living. Jesus said, 'If I then, your Lord and Teacher, have washed your feet, you also ought to wash one another's feet' (John 13:14). From home, family, friendship, acts of love and service, especially in any neighbourhood relationship of street, estate or work or church, we know that if our eyes are open, somewhere there will be need.

Remember the solemn admonition of Jesus during the Sermon on the Mount — just to help friends or greet them is not good enough; we must go further: 'Love your enemies and pray for those who persecute you' (Matthew 5:44). This is strong stuff — lived out it could change the face and heart of our society, our street, our homes, our congregation! Finally today we come to the supreme giving — Jesus giving himself in love, 'Take; this is my body.'

My only suggestion and plea is that we try to take Jesus at his word, in faith and love. Rather than being the great divisive issue between the Christian Churches, let us pray that the Eucharist may indeed become the sacrament of Unity. Let us come to understand each other in love between the Churches.

Prayer of Jesus   John 17:20–23.

MAUNDY THURSDAY

Gethsemane

And he came out, and went, as was his custom, to the Mount of Olives; and the disciples followed him. And when he came to the place he said to them, 'Pray that you may not enter into temptation.' And he withdrew from them about a stone's throw, and knelt down and prayed, 'Father, if thou art willing, remove this cup from me; nevertheless not my will, but thine, be done.' And there appeared to him an angel from heaven, strengthening him. And being in an agony he prayed more earnestly; and his sweat became

like great drops of blood falling down upon the ground. And when he rose from prayer, he came to the disciples and found them sleeping for sorrow, and he said to them, 'Why do you sleep? Rise and pray that you may not enter into temptation.'

(Luke 22:39–46)

We will concentrate today upon Jesus in the garden and arrested, because yesterday we thought about the Last Supper. Crucial is the little phrase 'as was his custom'. If we are to follow his way to the Cross by realizing it in our daily lives, we must grow to understand that Jesus had a custom of going to pray. It was not always in Jerusalem and the garden, but it was on lonely mountainsides, in the night, in the presence of his disciples, and so on. He also frequented the synagogue.

Again and again, I personally come back to the necessity of 'wasting time' on God in prayer. This is central in the following of Jesus on the way of the Cross. You might be able to follow on that way without prayer, but I do not know how you could survive!

We see Jesus in prayer in the garden. It is his ultimate 'kick' as a human being. At no point does he turn back from the way of his Father's will. But here he makes a strong human plea. We can feel the very real struggle. This should give us heart, especially when we read the scriptural record:

In the days of his flesh, Jesus offered up prayers and supplications, with loud cries and tears, to him who was able to save him from death, and he was heard for his godly fear. Although he was a Son, he learned obedience through what he suffered; and being made perfect he became the source of eternal salvation to all who obey him.

(Hebrews 5:7–9)

As we pray, and perhaps find that God seems very silent in answer to our pleas — consider Christ, his plea and the answer of the way of the Cross and crucifixion. Ask yourself what the writer means when he says: 'and he was heard for his godly fear'. For me this ties up with the foundation notion which comes in the next sentence: 'he learned obedience through what he suffered.' It may not be a pleasant thought, but we should think it out.

Now, after that prayer, Jesus is immediately confronted with the outcome of his prayer — namely that he was to go on through the bereavement of losing his followers, the humiliation of arrest instigated by his friend Judas, and the actual physical, mental and spiritual desolation of that night.

I am sure that you may have had to face desertion, or a feeling of doubt and desolation, an inability to pray, a sense that you have been let down. I can only say that you must keep on praying, because the Lord is very odd in his way of answering. It follows that we need some space, some silence, 'some waste of time' on God, to catch the cadence of his voice.

Meditation   The moon was caught in the branches;
Bound by its vow,
My heart was heavy.

Naked against the night
the trees slept. 'Nevertheless,
Not as I will . . .'

The burden remained mine:
They could not hear my call,
And all was silence.

Soon, now, the torches, the kiss:
Soon the grey of dawn
In the Judgement Hall.

What will their love help there?
There, the question is only
If I love them.

Dag Hammarskjöld (1905–1961)

GOOD FRIDAY
Jesus dies on the Cross

It was now about the sixth hour, and there was darkness over the whole land until the ninth hour, while the sun's light failed; and the curtain of the temple was torn in two. Then Jesus, crying with a loud voice, said, 'Father, into thy hands I commit my spirit!' And having said this he breathed his last. Now when the centurion saw what had taken place, he praised God, and said, 'Certainly this man was innocent!'

(Luke 23:44–47; cp. John 19:33–37)

What a day! If you really believe that Jesus Christ, born into this world of the Virgin Mary is not only her son but truly the Son of God, can you wonder at the description in St Luke about the darkness over the whole land? No matter whether it was an eclipse or something else, or even nothing other than imagination — the event in itself was enough to be what we sometimes call 'earth-shaking'.

Of course, it is difficult to come to grips with what depth of understanding there had been. Did anyone beyond the apostles and the women *really* begin to believe that Jesus was truly the Messiah? The answer should be 'yes'. But was it so? As for the chief priests, did they have a fear that this might be a challenge to them which went deeper than they could fathom — hence the attack on Jesus?

As we stand, sit or kneel at the Cross on this day of days, what are our thoughts to be? Believe me, you should be there and you should look on Christ crucified, and you should allow your mind to dwell there. I do not know what will emerge from within you. Nor do you! Leave it to God, and rely on his Spirit to guide you, his love to melt you.

Jesus has spoken from the Cross. He has asked his Father, 'Father, forgive them; for they know not what they do'. We could be included in that statement and request . . . we scarcely know what we are doing sometimes when we sin. We are caught up in our own purposes, which blot out everything and everyone else. That is what sin is like — the object becomes good to us, though bad in itself. But Jesus forgives us — and we can respond by sorrow, love and positive service.

Jesus had promised paradise to the thief who defends him and asks to be with him. Is this not an example for us? Jesus wants us with him, however bad, if only *we* want to be with him. His condition is our desire for friendship, love and closeness. As you are there — say from your heart — I know you love me! I am sorry I love you *so little!* Help me to love you more!

Another word has come from Jesus, a terrible and terrifying word: 'My God, my God, why hast thou forsaken me?' For us this is a most important cry, harrowing as it is. For we can come to that pit of despond where we seem to lose all hope. It is of immense importance that Jesus has tasted that depth. I have tasted it! Sometimes through my own fault, because I have been in the depth of sin and this has led me to feel cut off from God — but stupidly: in a way angry that he is not in touch with me as I wallow! Then there have been other times when I have been deeply in prayer, and he has disappeared, leaving me feeling utterly empty and bereft. I don't say I know what Jesus went through. Of course I don't. But I can know that he understands my small anguish.

Christ dies. On this day, nearly two thousand years ago, it must have seemed the end. Those solid, loving few stood by the Cross. Jesus himself said, 'It is finished' (John 19:30). If they heard that, what did they think

— the end? Or did they know he meant that he had done his Father's will to the end? He had finished the work he had to do . . . and as the other evangelist wrote: 'Father, into thy hands I commit my spirit!' (Luke 23:46).

Prayer   Psalm 22 [21]:1–5.

HOLY SATURDAY

✝ The body of Jesus is
XIII XIV taken down from the Cross and laid in the tomb

Now there was a man named Joseph from the Jewish town of Arimathea. He was a member of the council, a good and righteous man, who had not consented to their purpose and deed, and he was looking for the kingdom of God. This man went to Pilate and asked for the body of Jesus. Then he took it down and wrapped it in a linen shroud, and laid him in a rock-hewn tomb, where no one had ever yet been laid. It was the day of Preparation, and the sabbath was beginning. The women who had come with him from Galilee followed, and saw the tomb, and how his body was laid; then they returned, and prepared spices and ointments.

(Luke 23:50–56)

Many of us know the awful emptiness which follows death. The beginning of bereavement is painful and distressing. I have found that quite often there are two ways in which the bereaved person can react. Some are so numbed that they want to sit, weeping perhaps, not responding much to anything or anybody. Others find that their best hope, as they think, is to keep busy, so they make a lot of funeral arrangements, getting the family from far and wide, making sure there is plenty of food when they come.

We are told by Luke of the way the disciples occupied themselves immediately after Christ's death. But being Jewish, they were then faced with the long-drawn-out Sabbath, when there was practically nothing they could do, except prepare for a better tending of Jesus' body once the Sabbath was over.

92 *Holy Saturday*

There are different ways of coping with and even celebrating death in different countries. The Irish used to have wakes, but in England these seem to have faded. On the other hand, people with a Caribbean background normally gather at the home of the deceased very quickly, and for the nights before and after the funeral, there are long sessions of prayer, hymn-singing, sometimes eulogies of the deceased person, and refreshments for all who come. I have found this a very healing encounter, where tears can be shed, love exchanged, and the barrier of death made less absolute.

We have a real work of love to perform whenever we meet bereavement. This is especially important — because we have the fellowship of belief in Christ and his resurrection — if we are with other Christians. If we are with non-believers, our own faith and sympathy can penetrate, relieving pain and tension, without the need to preach. Often at that stage, presence is what matters. Often touch is a great comfort.

From the accounts in the evangelists, it must have been awful for the disciples and the women — more awful than for us (1 Thessalonians 4:13–14).

There is another lovely passage, which is in fact before the death and resurrection of Jesus, at the death of Lazarus, when Martha and Mary are in the desolation of bereavement (John 11:23–26).

We are confronted today with a certain amount of disbelief in the after-life. At the same time, there is growing interest in the occult, people searching the stars and using horoscopes, and so on. So it is urgent that our faith, and our living out of the approach to death and of coping with bereavement, should be strong supports for those with little or no faith. This means that we must be open ourselves to doubt, and open to the pain of loss, the emptiness of bereavement. In a sense, it is only through our own wounding that we can help to heal the wounds of others. None of us likes or enjoys going through bereavement, but when we realize that it does not get better after more than one, but rather worse, then we will be vulnerable enough to live through each death with a kind of dying in ourselves. This is followed by a kind of rising again, while we remain here on this earth, a shallow foretaste of the new life in Christ, but powerful in our distress.

Prayer   Psalm 130 [129].

✝ The Resurrection

They found the stone rolled away from the tomb, but when they went in they did not find the body. While they were perplexed about this, behold, two men stood by them in dazzling apparel; and as they were frightened and bowed their faces to the ground, the men said to them, 'Why do you seek the living among the dead? He is not here, but has risen.'

(Luke 24:2–5)

There is much discussion, and always has been, over the truth and meaning of the resurrection. No doubt it will go on. Our strongest statement from one of the witnesses of the resurrection, but not an eye-witness, is that of St Paul:

If there is no resurrection of the dead, then Christ has not been raised; if Christ has not been raised, then our preaching is in vain and your faith is in vain. We are even found to be misrepresenting God, because we testified of God that he raised Christ, whom he did not raise if it is true that the dead are not raised. For if the dead are not raised, then Christ has not been raised. If Christ has not been raised, your faith is futile and you are still in your sins.

(1 Corinthians 15:13–17)

Having tried to walk the way of the Cross during Lent, we burst into the glory of the Easter light. So bright is that light to our eyes of faith that it may well leave us in a dazzling darkness. We enter in to the depth of the mystery of God.

During the Easter season, try to read slowly the Bible stories of the event and the following weeks. Several things are striking. Firstly, it is to Mary Magdalen that Christ first appears. He tells her to go and tell his followers that he is risen. Women were the first witnesses when they went to the tomb; Mary was the first messenger of the good news. Secondly, faith remained very important in the acceptance of the resurrection of Jesus. None found it easy to recognize or accept Jesus in this after-death life. Even as late as the ascension of Jesus, 'when they saw him they worshipped him; but some doubted' (Matthew 28:17). This underlines our own continued need for faith, and our openness to doubt.

Thirdly, Jesus chose on many post-resurrection appearances to have a meal with his friends. A lot is said and sealed by eating together. Our main worship is the Eucharist, but we also need to be certain we are hospitable and have an open, family table. We come to know each other as well as Jesus Christ in the breaking of bread.

And so, after the way of the Cross, we are to live in the resurrection as Easter People, and know pain and falling and failure and even near-despair, but know also the merciful love of God, who has so loved the world that he sent his only Son. Amen. Alleluia.

Meditation   Romans 10:8–10.